GRACEFUL GOODBYES

A Pastors Guide to Delivering Impactful Eulogies
and Offering Comfort

IRA J. ACREE

LIFE TO LEGACY

Graceful Goodbyes
A Pastor's Guide to Delivering Impactful Eulogies and Offering Comfort
By: Ira J. Acree, Copyright © 2024

ISBN 13: 978-1-947288-79-9

Printed in the United States
10 9 8 7 6 5 4 3 2 1

Cover design by: Legacy Design Inc
                  Legacydesigninc@gmail.com

Published by:
Life To Legacy, LLC
20650 S. Cicero Ave, #1239
Matteson, IL 60443
(708) 272-4444
www.Life2Legacy.com

Table of Contents

ACKNOWLEDGMENTS

A special thank you to the committed members of Greater St. John Bible Church, whom I've been privileged to serve throughout my entire pastoral career, including those who are now among that great cloud of witnesses. The practical experience of doing life together—leading, teaching, and shepherding this amazing congregation—has been instrumental in shaping me as a pastor. Your love and support have been an essential part of my journey and have provided the wisdom and motivation behind the writing of this book. I am deeply grateful for each of you.

FOREWORD

I first crossed paths with Reverend Ira Acree back in 1999, right here in Chicago, at the Rainbow PUSH Coalition. He was a young, driven pastor, learning and serving alongside our mentor, Reverend Jesse Jackson. From that day on, I've watched him grow into a consistent and powerful voice in the civil rights movement. His commitment is unmatched, and what truly sets him apart is his relentless drive to take his ministry beyond the church walls.

I've seen him stand firm, even when others wouldn't. He's never been afraid to fight for justice, to speak up when it mattered most. Over the years, he's stood by my side during several eulogies I've delivered across the nation, showing the same fearlessness and compassion.

In Graceful Goodbyes, Reverend Acree draws from the depths of his calling—his shepherd's heart, his theological training, and his prophetic spirit—to offer critical guidance on a topic often overlooked: the delicate, sacred art of delivering eulogies. He reminds us that every life, no matter how it ended, carries value in the eyes of God. And with that, every eulogy must be handled with grace, dignity, and respect.

This book speaks to the seriousness of clergy being prepared to deliver words that honor the deceased and comfort the grieving. Reverend Acree's words will challenge every Christian to approach such moments with more care, understanding the weight of what we say to families in the aftermath of loss. Whether you're a young seminarian, a seasoned pastor, or a leader in the struggle for justice, this book will elevate the way you offer comfort in times of mourning.

Drawing from 35 years of pastoral ministry, Reverend Acree shares lessons from a range of experiences—eulogies for young victims of violence, pillars of his congregation, victims of police brutality, and beloved elders. He imparts pastoral wisdom, offering vital advice not only for ministers but for anyone seeking to support grieving families. He also shares crucial insights into what not to say, nuggets that will bless anyone from the seminary to the sanctuary to the streets.

In this work, Reverend Acree gives us all something invaluable: the tools to speak life, even in the shadow of death.

—Reverend Al Sharpton

INTRODUCTION

THE SACRED DUTY OF DELIVERING EULOGIES

Delivering eulogies, my dear friends, isn't merely about giving a speech; it is a sacred responsibility, a divine calling that falls upon the shoulders of every serious pastor or faith leader. It is not a task to be taken lightly, for we are given the profound duty of speaking the last words over a life that God Himself breathed into existence. Each eulogy is a testament to the life lived, a celebration of a soul that journeyed through this world, leaving behind footprints of life, love, and legacy.

When a pastor steps forward to deliver a eulogy, it must be with a heart full of compassion and a spirit attuned to the whispers of the Holy Spirit. The message should not be a one-size-fits-all recitation, but rather a deeply personalized tribute that resonates with the unique story of the individual who has transitioned from this earthly realm to eternity. Whether the person was tragically taken, fought a long battle with illness, or enjoyed the blessings of a long life, every circumstance surrounding their departure must be considered with sensitivity and respect.

We must remember that every life matters. Every soul that passes through our congregations and communities is a reflection of the divine image of God. Genesis 1:27 tells us, "So God created man in his own image, in the image of God created he him; male and female created he them." This profound truth underscores the intrinsic value and dignity bestowed upon each person by our Creator. It is this divine image that we honor when we stand before a grieving family and a mourning congregation to offer our final words of comfort and commemoration.

In crafting a eulogy, we are called to put the hay where the horse can get it, to make our words accessible and meaningful to those who hear them. Just as we would put the feeding trough where the cattle can reach it, we must ensure that our message of hope, love, and remembrance is within reach of every heart present. This is not merely about speaking eloquently; it is about touching souls, mending broken hearts, and lifting spirits.

We must acknowledge the manner in which the person transitioned, be it through tragedy, illness, or the natural ebb and flow of a long life well-lived. Each scenario carries its own weight, its own pain, and its own need for a specific kind of comfort and understanding. As men and women of God, we are entrusted with the sacred duty of delivering that comfort, of ensuring that every death receives a dignified send-off befitting the divine image in which each person was created.

As we fulfill this profound responsibility, let us do so with the reverence, compassion, and grace that it demands. Let our words be a balm to the wounded hearts, a light in the midst of darkness, and a bridge connecting the temporal with the eternal. For in every eulogy, we are not just saying goodbye to a life; we are honoring the divine creation of God, reflecting His glory, and celebrating the everlasting hope we have in Him.

A POWERFUL EULOGY POINTS THE LISTENERS TO CHRIST

A powerful eulogy should point the listeners to their hope in Christ. It cannot be reduced to a regular sermon, or you will miss an opportunity to provide hope during the time when it is desperately needed. Always remain sensitive to the fact that the grieving family and friends loved the deceased.

In my early years as a pastor, far too many times I apologized for not knowing the deceased and proceeded to preach a message that focused only on our hope in Christ. But that's tantamount to leaving the deceased out of their own eulogy. If you make that mistake, you run the risk of the family not hearing you. Be it right or wrong, their deceased loved one has their attention and has an unrelenting grip on their emotions.

No matter how gifted the ecclesiastical orator may be, the eulogy is not the time to showcase exegetical ability, nor is it the time to put on display your range of homiletical skills. In fact, far too many ministers deliver eulogies using the same time limit as their Sunday sermons. After 35 years, I can safely say, whatever your normal sermon length is, the eulogy should be half that time or less.

As the one delivering the eulogy, you cannot afford to blow this once-in-a-lifetime opportunity to talk about the precious life of someone who's very special to your audience. By the grace of God and His Holy Spirit, you will strategically use that person's life story to segue into speaking about the hope we have in Jesus; while emphasizing the grace He provides to give them strength. However, this message is not meant to minimize the pain death imposes but to help move beyond this difficult and dreadful immediate season.

In Matthew 5:4, the Bible says: "Blessed are those who mourn, for they will be comforted." The eulogist must not just quote this scripture; he must embody it as he performs his sacred duty. This is a time for empathy, a time for connection, a time to be a vessel of God's comfort. It's about wrapping the grieving in the warmth of Christ's love and showing them through the life of the one they've lost that hope in Jesus is not just a concept, but a living, breathing reality.

We must remember, a eulogy is not about us. It is not a platform for us to shine, but a moment to honor the life that has passed and to point the hearts of those in pain to the eternal hope that can only be found in Christ. We stand in the gap, lifting up the memories of the departed while gently guiding the mourners toward the comforting embrace of our Savior.

As eulogists, our duty is to be sensitive, compassionate, and succinct. To speak words that heal, to share stories that inspire, and to deliver the message of Christ's love in a way that resonates deeply within the hearts of the bereaved.

INTIMATE KNOWLEDGE OF THE DECEASED IS CRUCIAL

In my experience, eulogies are much more powerful and effective when the person speaking about the deceased knows them intimately. This is not to suggest that eulogies should not be delivered on behalf of a person that you don't know. If you're presented with that challenge, you can address it by doing your own diligent research about that person. Start by uncovering who they were, looking into aspects such as their occupation, the causes they championed or valued, the institutions they supported, and where they volunteered their service or time. It's crucial to delve into their hobbies and personal interests, as these details paint a fuller picture of their life.

As soon as you can, get an obituary. This document not only tells you about the person but also lists the people who were significant in their life. It's also vitally important to interview multiple family members and allow them to offer positive thoughts about their loved one. While you might want to use most of the information they provide, usually you won't. This process merely helps you better gauge the character and essence of the person you will be eulogizing.

Even when I know the deceased very well, I find it extremely helpful to interview family members. As a pastor, I realize that regardless of how much someone is honored and revered for their stewardship at the church, their life consisted of far more than their church membership. Their personal stories, family connections, and contributions to the community all enrich the narrative of their life.

When a eulogist knows the deceased, it adds a layer of authenticity and personal connection that resonates deeply with the mourners. Personal anecdotes, shared experiences, and a genuine understanding of the person's character bring a eulogy to life, transforming it from a mere recitation of facts to a heartfelt tribute.

The power of a well-delivered eulogy lies in its ability to capture the spirit of the deceased. It's about honoring their legacy and providing solace to those left behind. When you know the person, you can speak with a depth of emotion and insight that touches the hearts of the grieving in a profound way. You can highlight the unique qualities that made them special, recount moments that bring smiles amidst the tears, and remind everyone of the impact they had on the lives they touched.

Ultimately, whether you know the deceased or not, the goal remains the same: to celebrate their life, honor their legacy, and provide hope and comfort through the love of Christ. By approaching this sacred duty with humility, empathy, and a genuine desire to connect, you can ensure that your eulogy fulfills its purpose and brings light to a time of darkness.

WHEN THERE IS NOTHING GOOD TO SAY

Hebrews 9:27 says, "And it is appointed unto man once to die, but after this comes judgment." This verse is a stark reminder that we all have an inescapable appointment with death. That being said, can you imagine what's been the toughest sermon for me to preach throughout my career? For me, it's being put in the position of delivering the eulogy of an irreverent person of whom there is nothing good to say. It's such an undesirable position. Everyone is dressed well, on their best behavior, good music has been rendered, and you go through the protocol of the program. And then the lot falls on the preacher, where he has to fish for noble words to say about someone who has done nothing with "their dash."

The eulogist is supposed to get up and embellish and hallucinate a life that the deceased never lived. I have gotten to the point where I no longer put myself in that position. After praying, studying, researching, and interviewing friends and family, if no one can find anything good to say or find a contribution to humanity that the deceased has made, I can't do the eulogy. I'm willing to offer a scripture, a prayer, and even a song, but I won't do the eulogy.

For me, if I can't cry about the person I'm given the responsibility to eulogize, or at least be moved emotionally about their loss or a fond memory we shared, I feel like a very essential element is missing from my preparation, and I'm unfit. Somebody else can do the eulogy, or maybe some people shouldn't even have a funeral because there's just not much you can say about them.

Several years ago, a funeral occurred that I did not officiate, but it is the tragic story of a deranged young man who killed his entire family in the Chicago suburbs. Both parents were shot multiples times in their bedroom and his 18-year-old sister was strangled. He even killed the family dog. After committing this heinous crime, he flew to Florida and committed suicide in a motel room. Obviously, the funeral was gut wrenching. The three victims were funeralized together. However, for the deranged son that committed these horrific murders, there would have been nothing good to say.

Though this is an extreme example, it's a sobering truth that not everyone leaves behind a legacy worth celebrating. Some lives, for whatever reason, seem devoid of notable contributions or meaningful connections. When faced with such a task, it feels as though the very essence of the eulogy is compromised. How do you speak life and hope into a room filled with mourners when the life you're meant to honor feels empty or unremarkable.

This is not to say that every person must achieve grand accolades or societal recognition to be worthy of a heartfelt eulogy. Every life has inherent value, and sometimes, the quiet, humble lives are the ones that touch hearts most deeply. But when there is a complete absence of positive impact or memorable moments, the task becomes exceedingly difficult.

In these moments, I turn to God for guidance and discernment. I seek to find even the smallest glimmer of light in a seemingly dark narrative. But if, after all the prayer, study, and interviews, there is nothing to uplift or celebrate, I believe it is more honest and respectful to step aside. It is a heavy burden to bear false witness to a life not well-lived.

The purpose of a eulogy is to honor the deceased and provide comfort and hope to the living. It is not a platform for empty platitudes or fabrications. Therefore, when faced with the task of eulogizing a person who has left little to no positive mark, I choose to step back, offering my prayers and support in other ways, but leaving the eulogy to someone else. In doing so, I maintain the integrity of this sacred duty and ensure that the message of hope in Christ remains genuine and heartfelt.

1

Thirteen Things We Should Never Say to Grieving Families

Pastors, when dealing with grieving families, must be exceedingly mindful of their words to avoid saying anything that could be perceived as foolish or insensitive. It is crucial to approach these delicate situations with the utmost care and compassion, recognizing the intense pain and vulnerability of those who are mourning. One single thoughtless remark can deepen their sorrow significantly and cause lasting emotional harm. Therefore, pastors and faith leaders in general must strive to offer words of comfort and solace, rooted in empathy and understanding, to support and uplift grieving families during their time of need.

Over the years, I have heard a barrage of insensitive words spoken to grieving families. The list is endless, but I have compiled the top 13 worst things I've encountered during my thirty-five years as a lead pastor. These unfortunate remarks highlight the importance of choosing our words meticulously, especially in moments of overwhelming grief and loss.

1. **"I know how you feel"** is one of the most common comments made to grieving families, yet it is profoundly off base. One reason this remark is misguided is that no two people are the same. Everyone has the propensity to respond differently and distinctively to the same situations. Not only are no two people alike, but the conditions, context, and complexity surrounding every death are also unique. Everyone's grief journey is personal and shaped by their relationship with the deceased, their past experiences, and their emotional makeup. Thus, it is crucial to approach grieving families with empathy and an open heart, recognizing that their experience is uniquely their own and avoiding assumptions about their feelings.

2. **"This is God's will"** is, in my opinion, a heartless and arrogant statement to make to someone who has just lost a family member. I know it may be coming from a good place and the intentions are well, but the damage done can be catastrophic. There are two primary reasons for this. First, God's will can manifest as either His perfect will or His permissive will. This distinction challenges the notion that God is sitting back on His throne in heaven like a puppet master controlling everything we do. On the other hand, since permissive will enables flawed humanity to have a free will, you can never blame God for everything that happens on earth.

Understanding the complexity of God's will, we cannot be certain whether a death was caused by God's perfect will or allowed through his permissive will. Even if we were to reach heaven and discover that the tragic death of our loved one was indeed God's will, that's appropriate for heaven where God's purposes can be made manifest. However, here on earth, there is no rational reason or benefit in imposing such rhetoric on someone who's currently hurting abysmally from their loss. As it says in I Corinthians 6:12 (KJV), "All things are lawful unto me, but all things are not expedient." In times of grief, it is not expedient and rather reckless to make presumptive statements about God's will; rather, we should offer comfort and compassion, recognizing the complexity and mystery of divine providence.

3. **"You have to be strong for your family."** Another taboo phrase for a preacher to utter to a grieving family member is "You have to be strong for your family." This is a phrase that makes me grimace every time I hear it uttered to some poor hurting and helpless family member! Telling a grieving person to be strong can convey the message that their grief and feelings are not acceptable. It is unhealthy and inappropriate to encourage people to hold back their emotions and tears when facing something as grueling and exasperating as death. This can make them feel as though they are being asked to conceal their true feelings, adding an unnecessary burden during an already difficult time. Everyone has the right to grieve and to express their sorrow in their own way. Encouraging emotional honesty and vulnerability is far more compassionate and supportive, allowing individuals to process their grief in a healthy and authentic manner.

4. **"Your loved one is resting"** comforts very few families. In fact, this is the last thing I would want to hear if my 13-year-old daughter had been shot and killed in her home, like 7th grader Amaria Jones, who lost her life to a stray bullet in her Chicago Austin neighborhood back in 2020. No husband wants to hear empty platitudes saying his wife is resting shortly after she's passed away. Such a statement doesn't pass the smell test. Clearly, that's not the type of rest we are comfortable hearing about; otherwise, we would all be excited when our loved ones die. But, on the contrary, we want them to stay here with us indefinitely! The old saying is still true: "everyone wants to go to heaven, but no one wants to die." Therefore, let's find a way to extricate this phrase from our ministerial monologue. Instead of offering hollow comfort, we should make a concerted attempt to focus on being present, acknowledging the pain, and offering genuine support to those who are grieving. We must model this as faith leaders as well as teach it.

5. **"At least they lived a long life."** Far too many people make this foolish statement when an elderly person passes away. Even when someone loses a parent who happens to be 100 years old, the pain still cuts deep. I can personally attest to that. I remember when my great Aunt Annie was on her deathbed at 96 years old, no one could have told me how much her death would gut punch me. On the day she passed, the moment I received the call, I nearly went into cardiac arrest from the anguish of trying to process the finality of losing someone so dear to me.

Ironically, someone told me leading up to the funeral that it should be a happy occasion for our family, considering how long she lived and that she never suffered from an extensive period of illness. I understood what they meant, but the loss of this great woman, a grandmotherly figure, was so hurtful that I resented the comment to no end. We should never imply that people who lose older relatives forfeit their right to grieve, that's nonsense. Every loss is significant, and the longevity of a loved one's life does not diminish the pain of their passing one iota. Instead of offering dismissive platitudes, we should acknowledge the depth of the grief and the impact the deceased had on their loved ones. Grieving is a natural and necessary process, regardless of the age of the person who has passed away. We must honor that process with empathy and respect.

6. **"God always wants the best"** is no consolation for anyone to hear. There is nothing uplifting or inspiring about this pathetic and misleading theological idea that suggests your relative was so good that God couldn't wait for their natural death and prematurely took them on to glory. This notion seems to go against the nature of God. If God only wanted the best, it would also imply that thugs, gang members, hoodlums and the not so moral people are insulated from death. Obviously, that is not true.

Such statements not only distort the character of God but also offer no real comfort to those grieving a loss. Instead of resorting to these misguided adages and verbiage, we should focus on providing genuine support, acknowledging the pain, and affirming the worth and significance of the deceased's life. Grieving families need empathy and understanding, not hollow explanations that fail to address their immense sorrow. Love in action is a more accurate expression of empathy than any words we offer. It was President Theodore Roosevelt who once said "People don't care how much you know until they know how much you care." That wisdom still rings true.

7. **"Who's got the body?"** Sensitivity in words and timing after a loss is essential. In the immediate aftermath of the death of a loved one, grieving relatives often face a barrage of questions and concerns from friends and other family members. One common question is, "Who's got the body?" This inquiry aims to find out which funeral home has been entrusted with the deceased's remains. However, the choice of words and the timing of such questions are crucial.

When a person is grieving, particularly in the minutes and hours following a death, they may not be emotionally prepared to discuss funeral arrangements. The psychological adjustment to begin securing the services of a funeral director and establishment takes time. Prominent Chicago pastor, Dr. Marshall Hatch, a dear friend of mine, has often spoken about the insensitivity of this question. He recalls the moment his mother passed away, when he was only eight years old. Members of his faith community repeatedly asked, "Who's got the body?" For young Hatch, this phrasing was particularly jarring. He wasn't ready to hear his mother being referred to as "the body." His sarcastic response, "That's not 'the body,' that's my mother," highlights the emotional toll of such a blunt question. It was already difficult enough to grasp the reality of his mother's death, but referring to her as "the body" compounded his pain. This experience underscores the importance of choosing words carefully and being mindful of the timing when speaking to those who are grieving. Sensitivity and compassion should guide our interactions, ensuring that our words provide comfort rather than additional distress.

8. **Constant talking is taboo.** The Importance of silence and presence in times of grief is crucial. Constant talking is often taboo when a person has lost a loved one. It is better to say nothing than to say the wrong thing. There is absolutely no need to feel compelled to engage in continuous conversation; your presence speaks volumes.

Years ago, Reverend Leroy Elliott, a national evangelist within my faith tradition, was asked to offer words of inspiration to a family mourning the loss of a well-known pastor. While others before him delivered electrifying sermonettes, fiery speeches, and shared amazing stories, Elliott took a different approach, and his words shifted the climate of the room. He referenced Job's three friends—Eliphaz, Bildad, and Zophar—from Job chapter 2. He pointed out that these men erred by engaging in lengthy speeches that Job himself condemned and classified as unhealthy rhetoric. However, Elliott noted that Job's three friends did do one thing right that he greatly appreciated and admired: they spent time with him.

Job 2:13 states that they sat with him for the duration of seven days before offering any advice. They commiserated with their friend in silence. That action was very commendable. Reverend Elliott concluded his talk by saying, "That's all I'm going to do today. I'm going to engage in the ministry of presence. I'm going to spend the day with my friend." This story illustrates the profound impact of simply being present. Sometimes, the best way to support someone in their grief is through silent companionship, allowing your presence to convey your empathy and solidarity. I was glad I was there to witness his approach, it was a lesson that I tucked away in my spiritual knapsack and I've tried to apply appropriately.

9. **"You have a new angel watching over you."** The misguided comfort of you now having a new angel watching over you is rather morbid. The phrase "You have a new angel watching over you" is problematic on many levels. Firstly, it is theologically incorrect. There is nothing in the Bible that suggests our loved ones become guardian angels assigned to watch over us from heaven. This idea lacks biblical foundation and spreads a comforting yet inaccurate belief. The last person who should disseminate such spiritual poppycock is an ordained minister. I prefer to adhere to the theological concept Paul shares in 2 Corinthians 5:8, where he writes, "We are confident, I say, and willing rather to be absent from the body, and to be present with the Lord." This verse emphasizes that when believers die, they are immediately in the presence of the Lord, not assigned to guardian angel duties on earth. Furthermore, even if the notion were remotely true, it wouldn't suffice for most people. I know because I've heard many people reject that notion.

For years, I was deeply involved in gun violence activism in Chicago. On one occasion, I attended a prayer vigil standing beside a mother who had lost her son to gun violence. During the event, someone tried to comfort her by saying, "The silver lining in this grey cloud is that you now have your son as your new angel." The mother, overcome with tremendous grief, pushed back and insisted, "I don't need him as my angel. I want my son back! No, she screamed!" This poignant moment highlights the inadequacy of such statements.

Those grieving the loss of a loved one, the idea of their deceased becoming an angel often fails to bring solace. What they truly yearn for is the physical presence and companionship of their loved one, not a spiritual role assigned posthumously. Offering simplistic and theologically unsound platitudes can inadvertently deepen the pain of those mourning. In times of grief, it is essential that we provide comfort rooted in truth and sensitivity. We must be cautious with our words, ensuring they offer genuine solace rather than empty comfort. The promise of being present with the Lord, as affirmed in Scripture, provides a far more solid foundation for hope and consolation than the idea of loved ones turning into angels.

10. **"You should be rejoicing"** is a phrase that people sometimes have the audacity to say to grieving families. I wholeheartedly condemn the notion of this misguided urge to rejoice by people who should be offering comfort. These people often justify it with a Bible verse from Paul's letter to the Philippians, where he urged them to "Rejoice in the Lord always; again I will say, rejoice." While the apostle Paul encourages believers to have the spiritual maturity to rejoice in both good and bad times, quoting this scripture or making such a proclamation is not always wise when someone has experienced the death of a loved one. It's certainly not the ideal time to teach this principle.

The hope is that we will all grow in our faith to the point where we can find a way to rejoice even after the death of someone dear to us. However, it is not appropriate to preach this standard at grieving people. It's totally inappropriate and insensitive to shelve this theological concept down hurting people's throats. Imagine how bizarre and insensitive it would be for a mother to tell another mother, who lost her three-year-old child, like in the instance of Mekhi James, who was killed on Father's Day 2020, not to cry. Especially when the mother offering this advice has three children, all of whom are still alive. Well, that's easy for her to say when she's never gone to a morgue to identify her child.

Grieving families need compassion and understanding, not self righteous rhetoric that seems to diminish their pain. Mourning the loss of a loved one is a deeply personal and painful experience, and urging someone to rejoice during such a time can feel dismissive and hurtful. It is important to recognize and honor their grief, allowing them the space to mourn and process their loss.

In times of grief, it is more comforting to offer a listening ear, a shoulder to cry on, and words that acknowledge their pain rather than trying to rush them to a place of rejoicing. True spiritual maturity involves recognizing the appropriateness of our responses and providing support that is sensitive to the needs of those who are suffering.

11. **"God never puts more upon you than you can bear"** is another common phrase often stated to those experiencing trials and tribulations. It's frequently cited as though it's a Bible verse, yet I have not found it in scripture. Even if it were a biblical quote, it's not appropriate to say to people who have experienced a heart-wrenching loss because, quite frankly, most people aren't trying to hear that. For many, the pain, sadness, loss, and a sense of absence feel overwhelming and insurmountable.

In reality, God often does indeed put more on us than we can handle. Sometimes, in His sovereign purpose, He allows us to be crushed (Hebrews 12:4-12). He breaks us so that He can remake us, and He often impairs us to improve us. I often say that the waters, winds, and waves of opposition come into our lives not to drown us but to teach us how to swim. Think of how Jeremiah cried out in Lamentations because God had left his nation, city, and people utterly desolate and decimated.

My big brother Reverend James T. Meeks, the founding pastor of Salem Baptist Church of Chicago often tells the story of an overweight man trying to learn to swim at the beach one day. It didn't go well, and he nearly drowned, causing a horrifying scene. This heavyset man was kicking his legs and flapping his arms ferociously for some time, laboring and agonizing to survive. Meanwhile, an Olympic champion swimmer watched from the shore. People ran up to the swimmer, pleading with him to rescue the drowning man. He replied, "Okay, I'll get to him in a minute." This exchange happened three times.

Finally, the man exhausted himself, stopped kicking his legs and flapping his arms, and that's when the swimmer jumped in, put the man on his shoulders, and floated him to shore. When interviewed by the media later, the Olympic champion swimmer was asked why he waited so long. He explained, "I had to! Had I jumped in the water while that man was kicking and going crazy, we both would have drowned. When he couldn't go anymore, that's when I was able to step in and save him."

Brothers and sisters, it's the same way with the Lord! Man's extremities are God's opportunities. Sometimes the Lord waits until we can do no more, and then He steps in and saves the day. And when it's all said and done, the only one who can get credit is Him.

This illustrates an insightful truth: God often allows us to reach the end of our strength so that we can fully rely on His. When we are at our weakest, His power is made perfect in us. Rather than offering platitudes, we should acknowledge the depth of others' pain and point them towards the ultimate source of comfort and strength.

12. **"God Needed Him More Than You Do."** God needed him more than you do?" This may be the craziest of all the things you should never say to a grieving family. Let me put it this way: God is omnipotent, which means He enjoys unlimited power; nothing is too hard for Him. God can simply speak something into existence. Everything God wants to happen will happen; nothing can prevent His plans—not even our free will. God has power over life and death.

God is also omnipresent, which means He's everywhere all the time. Even if God decided to go somewhere, He would meet Himself coming because He's already there! Thirdly, God is omniscient, which means He knows everything. Given these incredible attributes, the premise that God needed your loved one more than you do is flawed. God doesn't need your loved one or mine for anything! God doesn't need anyone.

The Psalmist declares, "The earth is the Lord's and the fullness thereof, the world and they that dwell therein" (Psalm 24:1). He's omnipotent, omnipresent, and omniscient, so can we please stop telling people this homemade lie?

What God does need is for us to fulfill the Great Commission. He needs us to share our faith—that's one thing He has entrusted to us. It's our responsibility to witness, not His, as stated in Acts 1:8: "But you will receive power when the Holy Spirit has come upon you, and you will be my witnesses in Jerusalem and in all Judea and Samaria, and to the end of the earth."

This notion that God "needs" anyone diminishes His divine nature and provides false comfort. Instead, we should focus on the real hope and responsibilities we have. I urge us again, particularly those who have been called to the vocation of gospel carriers to be mindful of our words and ensure they reflect the true nature of God and His plans for us. Offering authentic, scripturally sound comfort will always be more valuable than resorting to well-meaning but misguided clichés.

13. Declaring **"This is a day of celebration"** at funerals can sometimes be highly inappropriate. While some services are indeed meant to be celebrations of a life well-lived, it is important to recognize that this sentiment is not always suitable.

I have pastored long enough to witness instances where the officiating minister chastised the congregation for not being festive enough. My parishioner Mary Graham's nephew, 16-year-old Elijah Sims, was tragically murdered. Elijah was a rising senior at Oak Park and River Forest High School, but was fatally shot while visiting his old neighborhood on Chicago's West Side, in the Austin area. His death hit home deeply because his parents had moved to Oak Park, a neighboring suburb, in hopes of providing a better life and future for their child. Yet, Elijah's life was cut short during a visit to his old community.

The family asked me to deliver his eulogy. The service was appropriately somber, reflecting the immense grief and outrage over the loss of a promising young life. Before giving Elijah's eulogy, I expressed my anger and sorrow at the senseless violence that claimed another young life. I emphasized that we must not normalize such tragedies or pretend they are acceptable. When we declare we are here to celebrate simply because the deceased was a good person or enjoyed life, we risk dishonoring their memory. We fail to show the righteous indignation warranted by their untimely and violent death. When a person dies in such a heinous and premature manner, it is not a time for celebration. Even as a veteran pastor, I sometimes struggle to maintain my composure during such funerals. The grief and sense of injustice are palpable, and it is important to honor those emotions.

Conversely, I have witnessed services that were upbeat and uplifting, celebrating the life of someone who lived fully, with their share of successes and failures in family and career. In these cases, celebrating their life feels appropriate and fitting, as it reflects a life well-lived and appreciated.

In conclusion, the tone of a funeral should be tailored to the circumstances of the decease's life and death. Sensitivity and discernment are crucial in determining whether a service should be somber or celebratory. Recognizing and respecting the grief and emotions of the bereaved is essential to honoring the memory of the departed.

I felt a sense of burden to share some insight on my top thirteen statements you should never make to a person or family that is grieving. These callous comments, though often well-intentioned, can inadvertently add to the pain of those who are mourning. As faith leaders, our role is to provide comfort and understanding, allowing grieving individuals to express their sorrow without judgment or unsolicited advice. For God's sake, let's be mindful of our words, so we can be exponentially better in supporting those in their darkest hours. Sometimes the best words are the ones never spoken.

2

THREE PILLARS OF A POWERFUL EULOGY

"The Title, Tribute, and Takeaway"

Please note that the insights I'm sharing in this chapter are drawn from my extensive experiences as a pastor and civil rights leader. I have eulogized individuals from various walks of life who passed away at different stages and from many disparate causes.

This segment is not intended as a lesson on homiletics; many who read this will already be accomplished preachers or well on their way to becoming one. However, preaching or delivering a eulogy requires harnessing a very special skill set. It is a travesty when a great spiritual orator fails a grieving family in their time of need by rendering a very ineffective eulogy. It may seem contradictory or even an oxymoron to suggest that a great preacher could actually fail at delivering a heart-stirring eulogy, but it happens more often than you'd imagine.

Even the most skilled preachers have struggled to find the right words to provide comfort, honor the deceased, and to offer hope to the bereaved. The emotional weight and unique nature of a eulogy demand more than just eloquence; they require empathy, authenticity, and a deep understanding of the human spirit. This chapter aims to illuminate the nuances of this delicate task, ensuring that every eulogy delivered can meet the needs of the grieving family and fulfill the speaker's own standards of excellence.

THE TITLE

Three elements have proven invaluable and essential in elevating the quality of my eulogies. First, I had to learn to be strategic in selecting the title. Rule out casually or haphazardly choosing your title without giving significant consideration to the personality, position, predicament, and other pertinent attributes of the person being eulogized. These intricate details will guide you and determine the nature of the title.

I often ask myself whether the title will primarily describe the person's celebrated life, highlight specific deeds or accomplishments that their life's work has championed, or serve as a communal call to action. Sometimes, when the grief is particularly traumatic and incomprehensible, the title can also provide a course of direction for those mourning.

By thoughtfully crafting a title that reflects the unique aspects of the individual, you set the stage for a meaningful and impactful eulogy that resonates with the audience and honors the legacy of the deceased.

The title of your eulogy gives you a fighting chance to capture the audience's attention. A great example of choosing a title that describes a life is one I share in this book, the eulogy of Mother Angelean Stockdale. I was determined to select a title that would honor this woman who modeled integrity and possessed impeccable character and grace as a wife, mother, and grandmother.

I perused a few passages of scripture that featured some of the bible's most powerful female heroes like Deborah, Esther, Ruth, Mary the mother of Jesus, and Hannah, but I kept coming back to Proverbs 31. In the end, I chose to tag that text with the title, "The Profile of a Godly Woman." This title encapsulates the essence of Mother Stockdale's life, highlighting her virtues and aligning them with the timeless qualities of a Godly woman as depicted in the scripture.

When my fellow high school alumnus and devoted choir member Vernitras Singleton passed away from cancer, I was resolved to select a eulogy title that would capture her devoted Christian life and stellar deeds as a witness for our Savior and Master. In the midst of grieving a lifelong friend and devout congregant, my mind was flooded with countless memories of her selfless sacrifices, the many souls she won to Christ, and the numerous individuals she either invited to our church or recruited into our church family.

The title I chose ironically emanated from a sermonic seed planted in my spirit years ago by my own pastor, Dr. Johnny L. Miller, as he eulogized a beloved member of his congregation. The title was a perfect fit for Vernitras and came from Acts 1:8, "A Faithful Witness." This title summarizes her unwavering dedication and the profound impact she had on our faith community, ensuring that her legacy of service would be remembered and honored.

When 29-year-old mother of two, Andris Breann Woffard, lost her life, allegedly fatally shot by her boyfriend, a Chicago Police officer, I knew the family needed more than just a pastor to conduct the service. They needed someone who could help give this case the much-needed media projection to ensure there would be no cover-up from a police department already under tremendous scrutiny for corruption.

I was committed to helping, but I also understood that the grieving and outraged family desperately needed pastoral support and direction. That's why I felt that Psalms 23 was the perfect scripture to anchor the message. I titled it "Getting Through The Valley." I sensed that this family would greatly benefit from the solace of a shepherd, a comfort that could only be found in the Great Shepherd himself, Jesus of Nazareth. The imagery used by David in this classic psalm was aimed at providing the family with the strength, hope and direction to navigate their profound grief and seek justice for Lady Andris.

Although I didn't know the deceased personally, I was certain that I was summoned to deliver the eulogy because of my high visibility in the community as a civil rights leader. This was also during the pandemic, when approximately 90% of churches were closed to in-person services, so this may have been another reason why the family selected me to deliver her eulogy.

In addition to preaching the sermon, I endeavored to support the family during this period of time in the valley. I held press conferences and issued statements to the media, demanding that Andris's killer be taken off the streets and brought to justice, even if the perpetrator was an active member of the Chicago Police Department.

During the unforgettable funeral service for 13-year-old Amaria, I undertook the near-impossible task of comforting the troubled family and their standing-room-only host of friends. I assured them that they were not alone and that her life mattered, which was the actual title of the message. We affirmed how precious, smart, talented and unique she was. The eulogy turned into a call to action as I implored the congregation and community to demand justice and ensure that the murderer of this young princess is held accountable and punished to the fullest extent of the law. The scripture reference for her eulogy was 1 Peter 2:8-9.

THE TRIBUTE

The second essential element that enhances a eulogy is including a powerful and personal tribute to the deceased. I concede that it is much easier when the person has lived a life that shows evidence of impact and service. There are many nameless and faceless heroes who have touched many lives, but their deeds are much more private. Their names never appear in newspapers, on the evening news, nor do they get recognized at church or win awards on their jobs. Sometimes, as I previously mentioned, we have to do the painstaking research on those who are being remembered, by interviewing those who knew them so that we can accurately tell their life story. It is imperative that you share the unique attributes that the deceased possessed and eulogize them with the dignity that their precious life deserves. The concept I'm addressing in this book, concerning the minister's sacred responsibility of delivering impactful eulogies, is deeply rooted in the biblical truth that all human life is precious.

I've found that paying heartfelt tributes to the deceased provides a measure of therapy for their family in many cases. Please note how personal stories and specific details resonate more deeply with those who personally knew the deceased, helping them feel a stronger connection and comfort. When the eulogizer puts the effort and his soul into preparing informed tributes instead of reducing the eulogy to a mere run-of-the-mill sermon, it blesses the people immensely. It helps to preserve memories and the legacy of the deceased, ensuring their memory is honored and cherished for generations.

I must reiterate: if the minister cannot put in the necessary time to prepare a personal tribute in the eulogy, it is better to decline the assignment. Allow someone who values the person's life enough to prepare thoroughly to properly highlight the importance of their life and the impact they had on others. After all, although the grieving process takes time and differs for everyone, most people only have one funeral. A well-prepared eulogy is not just a formality but a significant moment of honor and remembrance. It provides a lasting tribute that strives to comfort the bereaved and celebrate the unique legacy of the deceased. Therefore, it is crucial to ensure that the final words spoken over those we eulogize truly reflect their life, character, and the indelible mark they left on the world.

THE TAKEAWAY

The final element to enhancing the quality of the eulogy is a dynamic takeaway. The preacher must diligently ensure that the message provides hope to the loved ones of the deceased, and indirectly to the listening crowd who showed up to support the grieving family during one of the darkest moments of their lives. We must never forget the heavy burden we bear as clergy to leave the family with a glimmer of hope, even in the bleakest outlook. In the darkest and most dreadful times, words of hope can be a beacon of light, helping mourners find peace and direction amid their pain. For me, the takeaway is always hope. Pray and find a path to that panacea! This hope reinforces our spiritual beliefs about the afterlife, eternal rest, or reunion, offering assurance that death is not the end but a transition. This hopeful perspective is crucial in helping families and friends move forward with a sense of optimism.

The takeaway must be embedded in every eulogy that is delivered, whether it's for the 96-year-old church mother who lived a fruitful life beyond the normal life expectancy, the veteran basketball coach who passed from COVID-19 while in his prime, or the 13-year-old who was fatally shot in the sanctity of her home. Always offer Christ!

Sometimes, the hope we have in Christ assures families that they are not alone, even as they pick up the broken pieces of their lives in the aftermath of a heinous murder. They can always find solace in knowing that the perpetrators of the crime will face their due punishment, whether through the full weight of the law and criminal incarceration or ultimately by the hands of Almighty and Just God, whose eyes are in every place, beholding the evil and the good.

It is disingenuous on behalf of the minister and unhealthy for the grieving family to be told that they should not be angry. Anger is a natural part of the grieving process, especially when a loved one's life is unfairly snatched away by 'The Hope Thief.' Nevertheless, it behooves us to leave the family with hope. God has promised to bring good out of that which is fundamentally bad. Romans 8:28, assures us of this, stating, "And we know that all things work together for good to them who love God, to them who are called according to His purpose."

In conclusion, I can't emphasize enough how incorporating these three simple elements into my eulogies has significantly transformed and elevated their caliber and quality. I dare you to try it. It's simple: properly select a title that uniquely honors the deceased, invest time in preparing a personal tribute, and include a takeaway that provides hope. A unique title captures the essence of the person being memorialized, laying the foundation for a meaningful tribute. Personal anecdotes and specific memories bring the eulogy to life, connecting with the hearts of the audience. In my experience, offering a message of hope amidst the sorrow provides solace, helping those in intense grief find some level of peace and a sense of closure.

The sacerdotal role you fulfill in eulogizing congregants and the broader community is vitally important. Your words of wisdom, spoken as the final tribute to their loved ones, carry immense value. The opportunity to share the last words are not to be taken lightly; they serve as a source of comfort and guidance for grieving families, offering them solace during one of the most challenging times in their lives. Remember you are a vessel through which God may be working to preserve the sanity of those who are mourning.

3

A Select Group of Diverse Eulogies

𝕴 have had the honor of delivering countless eulogies over the past three decades. Some were like anything else in life—good, and others not so good. Ironically, some of the ones I personally thought were pretty good can't seem to be found in my archives. Hindsight is always twenty-twenty. Nevertheless, I openly confess that I have probably butchered a lot of eulogies down through the years because I was too young and inexperienced to grasp and implement the wisdom that I'm now trying to share in this book, which aims to help faith leaders more effectively deliver eulogies. Which helps families tremendously at such an emotional and traumatic time.

I've always had a hunger for knowledge, even as a young preacher. Unfortunately, despite all the classes, conferences, and conventions I attended, I don't recall receiving access to this precious and empowering information. This book is just a small remnant of eulogies that I was able to access while on a sabbatical granted to me by the Lilly Endowment. I would love to have included other eulogies that I believe were comforting and uplifting, but for some strange reason, I could not put my hand on them, and there are so many that this book couldn't contain them.

Full disclosure: for many years, I delivered eulogies and preached the majority of my sermons from notepads. In the early days, many were written on the back of manila envelopes, on the back of books, and on scratch sheets of paper. Oftentimes, I would write my messages and speeches on whatever I could get my hands on when the Spirit began to flow. In recent years, most of my messages are saved online, which is why I'm fortunate enough to share these.

There is a plethora of other messages we would like to share with you if the Lord allows us to do this again, and if, of course, many of you find value in this compilation of messages. This book contains thirteen eulogies, ten of which are for long-serving members of the church that I pastor, and whom I knew quite well. The remaining three were for two high-profile victims of Chicago gun violence at the time and a tribute to Reverend John Collins, and a dear friend who succumbed to cancer after a ferocious second bout.

Delivering a eulogy is one of the most sacred duties of a pastor. It requires not only the skill to speak eloquently but also the sensitivity to touch the hearts of the grieving. Over the years, I've learned that a powerful eulogy does not merely recount the events of a person's life but rather captures the essence of their spirit, their impact, and their legacy. It's about weaving together memories, emotions, and the hope we have in Christ to create a tapestry of comfort and inspiration. It's one of the most impactful sacerdotal services we will ever provide to our parishioners.

As I reflect on my journey, I recognize the importance of preparation, empathy, and authenticity in delivering eulogies. It's not just about what you say, but how you say it—how you connect with the mourners, how you honor the deceased, and how you point everyone to the eternal hope in Jesus Christ. This book is a testament to the lessons I've learned, the mistakes I've made, and the growth I've experienced as a pastor entrusted with the solemn task of eulogizing.

I pray that this compilation will serve as a guide and a source of inspiration for fellow faith leaders. May it help you navigate the delicate and profound responsibility of bringing comfort and hope to those who mourn. And should the Lord allow us to continue this work, I look forward to sharing more of these heartfelt messages with you in the future.

The Eulogy
for Mother Annie Mae White

I commend to you our sister Phoebe, who is a servant of the church which is at Cenchrea; that you receive her in the Lord in a manner worthy of the saints, and that you help her in whatever matter she may have need of you; for she herself has also been a helper of many, and of myself as well.
Romans 16:1-2, NASB

As we celebrate the life of this humble servant of God, I want to underscore an instance in scripture wherein a selected number of unsung heroes of the faith are heralded and recognized by the great Apostle Paul. In the 27 verses of this chapter, more than 30 different names make the honors list.

The Title:

You Don't Have To Be A Star To Be In God's Show

I. The Extraordinary Ordinary

These are nameless and faceless people who Paul commends for their significant impact on his ministry.

He could have called the names of the big time larger than life biblical figures and the high-profile celebrity type Christians of the early church era.

Silas would have been one I would have expected him to reference. He was his prophetic partner in crime. They did significant work for the kingdom together.

Titus was one of Paul's popular Greek protégés and one of his star-studded students. Titus is a significant figure in the New Testament. Titus accompanied Paul to Crete where he helped organize a church there. Though he was a mentee of Paul, and an epistle is addressed to him, nevertheless, he didn't mention his name.

Peter, (The apostle who is believed by many to have been the first pope of the church) as important as he was Paul was not moved to put his name in this special group that he is giving his highest commendations.

As you read through this diverse group of names there is something that is quite noteworthy.

No apostles are on his list.

No author of any of the New Testament books made his list.

No one on the list had a building erected in their honor.

They were not household names on the list.

However, without these nondescript individuals, Paul's ministry would have been an abysmal failure.

Even as prominent and influential as Paul is today, it is because of the impact and contribution of obscure and virtually unknown committed believers that he has maintained such a prolific position in the realm of Christianity throughout history.

Likewise, some of us wouldn't be known by many of you today had it not been for the soul winner and saintly touch of Mother Annie Mae White's hand in our lives.

The Tribute

Last week the legendary and renowned film critic Roger Ebert passed, and his death received international attention from people all across the globe. Today the life of Mother White a servant of God, is being funeralized and obviously she didn't get the same media splash as Mr. Ebert.

That's precisely why this passage inspires me so much!

EMPHASIS

Some people don't have big names, but they have big deeds!

Mother White's not as famous as: Sojourner Truth, an African American abolitionist and women's rights activist!

She didn't have the prominence in history as Harriet Tubman who developed the Underground Railroad that put many Black people on the right track to freedom.

She didn't have the notoriety of a Fannie Lou Haymer, a prominent civil rights activist known for her work in the struggle for voting rights and her role in the civil rights movement!

She's not in history books like Rosa Parks, the one who sat so Dr. King could walk!

She's not as celebrated as: Mae Jemison, Oprah Winfrey, or Michelle Obama!

The president, the governor, or the mayor may not know her name, but I'm grateful that the King of King and The Lord of Lord does. The Lord of glory knows her name!

What distinguishes these personalities of our text are the same attributes that made Aunt Annie such an outstanding impactful Christian woman, a virtuous woman, a woman of character, the very image of a godly woman.

II. SHE WAS A DEDICATED SERVANT

These names found in Romans 16, are being revered because of them going the extra mile for the kingdom.

Paul didn't just call their name, but he gave context for their commendations underscoring the significance of their contributions.

Starting in verse 1, with Phoebe, a great servant of the Lord, in whom Paul attested that she has been a great help to himself and many people.

Verse 3, Aquila and Priscilla, Paul praises them for risking their lives for him. This courageous couple opened the doors of their home and showed hospitality within an environment of hostility and allowed Paul and his congregants to have church within the walls of their humble abode.

Verse 7, Paul made sure that everyone knew to "greet Andronicus and Junias, my relatives who have been in prison with me."

This is just a small sampling in a great chapter that millions of Christians have read throughout the centuries. These precious souls have gone on, but their names live on. Indeed, Paul gives a few accolades and that-a-boys for people who had gone the distance for the kingdom and him! In essence what he is really saying is they were beyond the norm! In his book they make the esteemed Kingdom's honor roll.

ILLUSTRATION

Aunt Annie, as many of us affectionately call her, was proud of me for my academic achievement growing up. At least most of the time she was. Well that being said, there is a big difference between making the honor roll and getting a D for a grade! See, you can basically just show up and do the bare minimum and get yourself a D, but to get an A, you have to go the extra mile!

EMPHASIS

That's the type of person Aunt Annie was, she went the extra mile as a neighbor! She went the extra mile as a relative!

She went the extra mile even as a church member!

Many church people today want special recognition for just showing up!

She wasn't just a "show up" only member! The day she joined this church she was all in. She selflessly gave her time, talent and treasure to support this institution!

I would not be the pastor and civil rights leader that I am today without her investment!

I submit to you today that Paul remembers these people because they were there for him during the most impressionable and vulnerable moments of his life. You don't forget people who were there for you during those moments! Some people will promise to be with you through thick and thin, but when it gets thick, they thin out.

Paul says it's hard to forget people who were not just in your cabinet but were in your corner! In your corner When you were sick!

In your corner when your back was up against the wall!

In your corner when your spouse walked out on you!

In your corner when your money was funny and change got strange! You can't forget folk who let you stay in their home and eat their food!

𝕿𝖍𝖊 𝕿𝖆𝖐𝖊𝖆𝖜𝖆𝖞

I don't know if you told Mother Annie White before she took her flight, but some of you remember her for being there for you when you migrated here from other parts of the country.

You remember her letting you stay in her home when you had nowhere else to go!

You remember her loaning you money! You remember her babysitting your kids! (I'll raise my hand right there.)

You remember her being that friend through thick and thin. She told you the truth, whether you liked it or not.

She mothered many children even though she never birthed a child.

I remember her providing many firsts for me!

She took me on My first airplane ride to see my maternal grandfather, which was her brother, down in Okeechobee Florida.

At 10 years old, she opened my first bank account and it's still open. I eventually got over $100 in that joker!

She purchased my first organ and there's a long story behind that. She saw me overreacting at another relative's house like I had never seen an organ. So, she went and bought me one and before you know it I was enrolled in music school.

It was nothing but the love of God that allowed her to love so unself-ishly and unconditionally!

Today we celebrate a virtuous woman. However, Ebony Magazine, may not be here to commend her. Her name may not appear in Essence or Jet Magazine editions this week, but I'm glad that it made it to the Lamb's book of life!

I remember what my late pastor would sing when I was just a young boy, "I'm glad salvation is free! If religion was a thing that money could buy, the rich would live, and the poor would die!

If you're here today, let Aunt Annie's life be a lesson to you!

You don't have to be a star, to be in God's show!

All you have to do is come unto Jesus, the author and finisher of our faith.

I can hear him today in this home-going service of our dear church mother: "Come unto me, all ye that labour and are heavy laden, and I will give you rest (Matthew 11:28). You will need Him, because Auntie is gone! You can't run to her house anymore! If your life is a wreck, you can draw from her teaching but you can no longer access her counsel.

When I was a young driver traveling along the highway, I used to think that all the highway patrolmen knew how to do was to write tickets for speeding! I used to get so upset and nervous whenever I would see one parked or riding along the road, because of my para-noia! But I later found out that he was also cruising for crisis.

If you ever have an accident or problems along the freeway, all you gotta do is let up your hood and tie a white rag on the antenna and the highway patrolmen will come to your rescue and get you back rolling again! Well, it's the same way with the Lord Jesus! As we say so long to Mother White, always remember although she's not with us, if we wreck our lives, if we get stuck along the way, if we make the wrong turn and lose our direction, if you call on Him, He'll get you rolling once again.

THE EULOGY
FOR BREANN WOODFORD

The LORD is my shepherd; I shall not want. He maketh me to lie down in green pastures: he leadeth me beside the still waters. He restoreth my soul: he leadeth me in the paths of righteousness for his name's sake. Yea, though I walk through the valley of the shadow of death, I will fear no evil: for thou art with me; thy rod and thy staff they comfort me. Thou preparest a table before me in the presence of mine enemies: thou anointest my head with oil; my cup runneth over. Surely goodness and mercy shall follow me all the days of my life: and I will dwell in the house of the LORD for ever.
Psalm 23:1-6, KJV

The Title:

Getting Through This Valley!

After more than three decades as a pastor, it's very rare that I find myself at a loss for words. There are no words for grief of this magnitude. We are here together, wordless, numb, and hurting. It's virtually impossible to make sense of this senseless loss. But we have congregated to pay homage and respect to one of our best and brightest stars.

Breann modeled education for her children, her family and for other young women!

Her death is sad on a number of levels. It appears to be a breach of trust of epic proportions! It's incomprehensible to try to make sense out of nonsense!

Our collective hearts are broken for this family as we prematurely say goodbye to this young princess!

Before some super saint suggests otherwise, let me assure you that it's okay to cry! Don't let anybody tell you to play like you're happy during horrific inexplicable moments like these that occur in your life.

We can cry expressing our grief, while crying and demanding justice at the same time! Don't get it twisted!

It's more than the Young and Wooford families who are upset this afternoon regarding her senseless death! The Austin community is upset! I dare to say considering the nature of this homicide many in the city of Chicago are downright angry!

We want charges and convictions for this case!

Criminals should go to jail regardless of whether they wear blue suits or blue jeans!

There is no excuse for this beautiful young woman with two loving children to be taken away from us so soon! Oh, what a valley!

David uttered these uplifting words some 3000 years ago, yet it applies personally to us today. "The Lord is my shepherd."

David was a shepherd with status, stature and stardom, but he admitted that he encountered dangerous valleys along His journey. Life itself is filled with so many dark, dangerous and deadly valleys.

I. A DARK PATH

Verse 4, "Yea thou I walk through the valley of the shadow of death...."

To drive home his point, David uses imagery from a literal valley in Palestine. David was quite familiar with valleys, because he was a shepherd boy. These places are dangerous and deadly!

David teaches us invaluable lessons that we can use when we encounter the dark paths of life. Heavy emphasis on the word *when*, because if you keep on having birthdays you will most definitely face your share and a plethora of dark paths along your journey.

Science put a lot of time and resources behind research and discovering a Covid vaccine, and rightfully so. Oh, how I wish it were possible to discover a vaccine that could shield humanity from the agonizing storms of life! Imagine if such a vaccine existed—one that could protect us from the emotional and psychological hardships that inevitably come our way.

You can read your bible daily, support a wonderful charitable cause, and pray for an hour every day, but you will never be immune from the trials, trauma and tragedies of life's valleys or the shadows of death that accompany it.

The Tribute

II. His Divine Presence

Verse 4b "...I will fear no evil, for thou art with me!

Don't surrender or acquiesce when you're faced with the inevitability of life's storms and struggles.

Family, press on and keep on fighting! Please try not to get bogged down with worry!

Don't you forget that the good shepherd is with you! (Psalms 24:7)

Illustration

There's an old story about a little boy who was so frightened by a storm one night. Several times he cried out in fear and his mother would come to his room to comfort and to remind him that God was always with him. As she prepared to leave his room for the third time, her son grabbed her arm, held it tight, and said, "I know Mommy, but I want God with skin-on him!"

Family in the midst of your tears, you've had appearance after appearance from strangers and friends, that's "God with skin-on." I suggest to you today that perhaps in a small measure God has manifested himself to this family as a God with skin on!

"God has skin-on" when you've been blessed to have people of all faiths and ethnicities standing with you offering prayer and giving support.

"God with skin-on" is having the backing of civil rights leaders, activists and upstanding police who will call out rogue cop activities.

"God with skin-on" is having people present in your dark valley with hugs and handshakes, laughter and tears, conversation and quiet when those dark and difficult days come and it seems as if the nights get longer.

David assures us whenever we are in a valley, that a mountain top is ahead.

A valley is only a signal that I'm in between mountains!

Your journey is not complete, you will get through this valley! It's hard to grasp it now, but God has not forgotten about you. The psalmist assures us that God is our refuge and strength, a very present help in trouble, Psalms 46:1.

I'm glad that we serve a God who can bless you even in your valleys!

III. HE'S A DYNAMIC PROVIDER

He prepares a table. Before me is a preposition of location or an adverb of time!

Eating in that culture was an event!

It wasn't like today where everyone gets their plate, and everyone heads to their room with five different televisions playing. No, Eating was a time of fellowship and sharing! You could talk about your personal concerns, or how your day went or even current events that were going on in the world.

Entrees would be prepared to the diner's delight in their presence.

ILLUSTRATION

Some of you may have been to Benihana, it's a unique restaurant with a Japanese theme. You sit at a table, and a guy comes out with his knives and he's cleverly throwing them through his legs, and behind his back, flipping them and catching them without losing control. He's a craftsman and an artist, and He begins to actually prepare the meal right in your presence. He brings out the hors d'oeuvres, the shrimp and the meat and He begins to slice and dice and make it nice, right before your eyes.

Here's the catch, as exciting as things appear, this is only the beginning! You know the main entree is coming. Even though you're watching him go through all the preliminaries and preparing the appetizers, in your mind you still know a main course is coming!

Emphasis

That's the way God works, sometimes He puts you in the position where you can smell a blessing coming!

He's a dynamic provider!

God works through people! God's going to provide for them!

Through people. Dominican University you stepped up. City of Chicago now it is your turn to step up and provide for these two children!

If it's true that one who took the oath "to serve and protect," cowardly took this young woman's life! If it's true now!

Two little innocent children should never ever have to worry about where they will lay their head!

Dependable Protector!

God has you covered on every side!

Verse 4...He's with me, thy rod and they staff comforts me

He prepares a table before me in the presence of mine enemies!

He anoints my head with oil!

My cup runneth over. Surely goodness and mercy shall follow me all the days of my life and I will dwell in the house of the lord forever.

As my shepherd he's in front of me!

And The shepherd has a rod on one side of him, and a staff on the other side of him!

Then Goodness and mercy is following me. In essence goodness and mercy is chasing me, pursuing me, and covering me!

I still don't think y'all caught it! Let me say it a little louder for the people in the back! Goodness and mercy is chasing me, pursuing me, and covering me! Then I got the Holy Spirit inside of me!

So don't let discouragement hold you down or distress keep you down, and don't let depression tie you down!

Keep the faith, because God can lead you through your valley!

The Takeaway

I have run many 5K events down through the years with the United Negro college fund! I was so glad to support this annual initiative through my longtime friend, retired officer Carla Johnson of the Chicago Police. Running this race was sometimes humiliating! You know why because there were always so many much better, agile, and quicker runners in the race than me! So many who start off with me pass me by! The last year that I ran, Officer Johnson beat me and was sitting down drinking Gatorade, when I arrived at the finish line. I almost quit because of that frustration, but I kept on pushing!

Knees were sore, wind was short! Discouraged! But I kept pushing! Sweating profusely! The best part about the race however is the reception you get when you finish the race! People who finished the race before me, were congratulating me and welcoming me! And so it is!

The other day Breann completed her race! As tough as it is for us on this side, there is a celebration going on right now on the other side. I can see so many of her loved ones waiting at heaven's gate saying welcome home! Both of your grandfathers will be waiting, and your grandmama will be too, saying welcome home my child. Nevertheless, most of all King Jesus will be there saying "welcome home." Well done thy good and faithful servant. Enter into the master's joy!

THE EULOGY OF
MICHAEL "COACH DUBB" WILLIAMS

For you have not received a spirit of slavery leading to fear again, but you have received a spirit of adoption as sons by which we cry out, "Abba! Father!"
Romans 8:15, NASB

The Title:

Terms of Endearment

A few weeks ago, I faced the daunting and disheartening task of eulogizing a 13-year-old girl who lost her life after being gunned down in her own home while dancing for her mom to a Tik-Tok video. Though all deaths are traumatic, the difference between the 13-year-old's and today's service could not present a more stark contrast.

Today, we gather to celebrate the life of a remarkable man who dedicated his life to fulfilling the purpose God placed upon him: coaching and instructing our youth. His unwavering commitment and passion for guiding young minds have left an indelible mark on all who had the privilege of knowing him.

Today, my brothers and sisters, we celebrate a true man! Not a dude, not a deadbeat dad, not a player from the Himalayas, but a man who taught young people to put hope in their brains, not dope in their veins!

The text I chose for this message is intentional because it contains a specific term that gives the necessary emphasis that encapsulates the life of this great man who impacted so many lives. The text reads as follows,

> The Spirit you received does not make you slaves, so that you live in fear again; rather, the Spirit you received brought about your adoption to sonship. And by him we cry, *"Abba*, Father." (NIV)

This term of Aramaic origin has particular significance in its nuance as a term of endearment. In our English vernacular it is equivalent to our intimate term "daddy."

Terms of endearment are words we use to address people that we love or have special affection for!

All of us are familiar with them!

One of the most popular ones of this era is Boo!

Sweetheart, Sugar and Baby are very common terms of endearment!

Terms of endearment are not just limited to the realm of romance, but families also have these affectionate names for each other.

Pooky, Baby Sis, Baby Bro, June Bug, Homie! How about Peaches? Anyone named Peaches or Sweet Pea here today?

I don't care how old you get. If an Auntie gave you a nick name as a child, just come around her as a grown up. She'll still call you that same name 25-years later. That's because terms of endearment transcend time, because they come from the heart giving emphasis to a special connection between you and them. Let someone else call you by that same name that Auntie called you, and the reaction would be different! That's Auntie's exclusive term of endearment. It's okay for her to say it, but no one else can get away with it!

The Tribute

"A Man Called COACH"

Mike was affectionately called Coach Dubb!

Mike and I share many mutual friends. We attended Steinmetz High School during a time when there were not many folk like us around. Later, he joined our church, giving me the honor of being his pastor. Coach is well-respected all over the country and is affectionately known to most as Coach Dubb. To emphasize and encapsulate Coach's impact on so many lives, I have developed the following acronym.

C–Stands for "Compassionate"

In the dictionary, right next to the word compassionate there ought to be a picture of Coach Mike "Dubb" Williams! He embodied the words of scripture:

"Be kind and compassionate to one another, forgiving each other, just as in Christ, God forgave you (Ephesians 4:32).

No one would ever expect such a kindhearted spirit to be residing inside this big tall burly loud mouth man! (And Oh, was he loud!) But guess what? You couldn't let that put you off because he would give you the shirt off his back! He was always on the giving end!

Since 2001, our church has given away thousands of dollars annually to support local college students. Coach Dubb always supported my scholarship efforts, even before he officially became a member of our congregation. He was about love in everything that he did. Coach was a compassionate man!

O–Stands for "Old School" (His wife had another "O" word, outstanding!)

Coach was old school in everything!

Old school music!

Old School man!

Old school Church!

Old School coach!

He didn't believe and even swore that most players in this era could not play or compete with the athletes who played in the 80's and 90's because they were all about themselves.

"Coach was special. Different and unique he was indeed, but his way—the Coach Dubb playbook—worked! He was successful!"

A–STANDS FOR ATHLETIC (COACH WAS AN ATHLETE!)

Sports were his passion! It was his panacea for his problems, but it was also the path to his purpose!

He was an exceptional Athlete and expected nothing short of excellence from his players!

I don't think there is a person on earth who loved Kobe Bryant any more than him! The tragic death of the Black Mamba left a hole in his heart. We both were Laker boys and Kobe fans and grieved as if we knew him personally.

During the NFL and NBA seasons, no one could talk as much smack and trash talk as Coach Dubb if the team, he was rooting for was winning. His spirited banter and sharp wit kept him in the center of a sports argument. Coach Dubb's enthusiastic and often humorous jabs kept everyone entertained.

He gave his life to this! He knew the game so well and he gave his heart and soul to it!

ILLUSTRATION

He gave us all that he had.

Dr. King said It does not matter how long we live but it's how well you live!

The late Reverend Myles Monroe, a Bahamian pastor and Christian author once said "...Don't die old, die empty. That's the goal of life. Go to the cemetery and disappoint the graveyard."

C-STANDS FOR COMICAL

Coach was comical. Proverbs 17:22 "A cheerful heart is good medicine, but a broken spirit saps a person's strength" (NLT). I'm not trying to suggest to y'all that Coach was a bible scholar by any stretch of the imagination, but he must have read and cherished this verse!

Coach Lived, loved, laughed and looked up every day of his life!

The late legendary basketball coach Jimmy V. used to say "If you laugh, you think, and you cry, that's a full day. That's a heck of a day. You do that seven days a week, you're going to have something special."

He lived his life! Coach had an incredible ride, doing exactly that.

Each of us should take a page from his book of life! Make sure that you make your life count!

Hebrews 9:27, states "...inasmuch as it is appointed for men to die once and after this *comes* judgment" (NASB). This is the realest verse you will ever find! We all have an inescapable appointment! Death is the universe's greatest human equalizer! Whether we are black, white, Asian or Hispanic, rich or poor, liberal or conservative, we all meet at the grave as equals. The grave has no more respect for Jeff Bezos, the multi billionaire Amazon CEO than it does for you, me, or Coach.

Illustration

Me and Coach came up in the era where Monopoly was a popular game!

I used to love playing Monopoly when I was growing up! As a poor boy, it thrilled me to own all the properties, especially Boardwalk and Park Place. I would flat out get an adrenaline rush when I had sets of properties with four houses and a hotel, and then have the pleasure of one of my cousins landing on my property and having to pay up! And by no stretch of the imagination was I going to have any mercy. And I wasn't going to be satisfied until I could win it all, taking every last, house, railroad, and building.

During the game, I was in my glory, but at the end, the fun was over, and so was my gloating and bragging because all the riches that I accumulated all went right back into the box. Everything—every house, every hotel, every title, every utility, every railroad, and every dollar—went back into the box.

Here's what I'm saying! So it is in life; you can't take any of this stuff with you! A more poignant lesson is that it all goes back in the box.

Although players come and go and there are always winners and losers, in the end, it all goes back in the box. In life, everything we possess that we are so proud of—titles, houses, cars, and fat bank accounts—we can't take them with us when our bodies turn cold and go into the box. We must remember that what really counts is what we do for Christ. Coach went to church, but he knew that the best way to serve God was to serve his fellow man. He invested his life in people and not mere possessions.

H—STANDS FOR IS FOR HONORABLE

This morning here lies a man! A Good Man, and honorable man!

Family! This man loved you!

He loved his mama! His dad! Toya, he loved you! Gab and Tawanda, you were his life. Tawanda, He thought you were the perfect wife for him. It's one thing that got on his nerves. It was your behavior and the excessive over the top praise you displayed in church. He wanted you to be more laid back like him.

Friends! He was loyal to us

Faith! He lived his faith!

That's good too, because "...the just shall live by faith." Coach Mike Dubb William walked by faith every day of his life.

I often told Coach that we both are ministers! We both were changing and shaping lives. The primary difference was my sanctuary was the church, his sanctuary was the stadium.

There has got to be a special section in heaven for people like Coach! I wonder sometimes if there are box seats in heaven, because this guy deserves special treatment.

There will be 3 big surprises on judgment day! The first big surprise will be, there will be some folk there you don't expect to be there. The second big surprise is that you will be looking for some folks, who won't be there. The third biggest surprise is that some of you will wonder how in the world did you end up there. Just kidding. I threw that one in for Coach.

The Takeaway

In my closing, I urge you my friends, to be like Mike! Not MJ. But like Coach Mike Dubb Williams.

ILLUSTRATION

Pastor Tony Evans often talks about his fear of elevators. There was something about riding up and down in a little box several hundred feet off the ground that has never sat well with him. He worried that something would go wrong. One day it did. The car he was riding in got stuck in between floors way up in the higher floors. He noted that some of the people in the car became frantic. They began to beat on the door hoping to get someone's attention. Others began to yell in the hopes that their voices would get someone on the surrounding floors to come to their aid. But nobody heard their noise or their cries.

Then Evans quietly made his way to the front of the car, opened a little door in the wall and pulled out a telephone. Immediately he was connected with someone on the outside. He didn't need to beat on the wall to get their attention. He didn't need to speak loudly on the phone to receive their help. He could have whispered and they would have heard him. In this world, we're going to get "stuck" in places we aren't comfortable with. Some people begin to beat against the walls, others cry out in dismay. But the person who trusts in the power of confident prayer knows there's someone on the other end who answers their call and comes to their aid.

Family I know your heart is heavy today! I won't tell you not to cry! I won't tell you to celebrate! I won't tell you that I know how you feel! One thing I know is that you're in an uncomfortable spot. So many people tell you to rejoice, but it's easier said than done. Death hurts! But I want you to remember that Jesus is on the main line! And you can tell Him what you want! Call Him up and tell Him what you want! I'm a living witness He will come to your rescue!

Paul called him Abba, which is like calling him daddy! The song writer says some of y'all call him Mary's baby, Wonderful Counselor, Mighty God, but to me He's Jesus.

And finally, when you consider the greatness of our God, the sovereign of the universe, the creator that spoke everything into existence. He's not some far away deity detached from His creation, who cannot be touched with the feeling of our infirmities, but He is a loving and caring God, that sticks closer than a brother, and is a present help in a time of need.

We don't need any official protocol or special connections to reach Him. We don't need any secret password to access Him, but all we have to do is utter our term of endearment, "Daddy." Aint got time for the Hebrew. Don't need to know any Greek, just the simple word "Daddy" will get you through.

Coach Mike Dubb Williams has finished his leg of the race and taken his seat in the stands with the great cloud of witnesses. He's cheering us on that no matter how hard it gets, or no matter how bad it hurts, we can make it!

Family and friends, gathered here today, I have one last parting message for you—stay in the race. Don't stop now. We've come too far to turn around now. Run your race with patience, stay the course and finish your game. Until we meet again, be assured that those who are in Christ Jesus, like Coach Mike Dubb, we all win in the end!

THE EULOGY OF
DEACON ADREW BETTS

For those who are led by the Spirit of God are the children of God. The Spirit you received does not make you slaves, so that you live in fear again; rather, the Spirit you received brought about your adoption to sonship. And by him we cry, "Abba, Father." The Spirit himself testifies with our spirit that we are God's children. Now if we are children, then we are heirs—heirs of God and co-heirs with Christ.

Romans 8:14-17

The Title:

Term of Endearment: DEAC

It was April 11, 2020, less than one month after the country had been shut down as a result of the Covid 19 pandemic. It didn't take long for our church to be hit with the reality of this invisible enemy that took the lives of more than 4.5 million people worldwide, during the pandemic. We lost a trooper, our beloved Deacon, Mr. Adrew Betts on Palm Sunday, April 5th.

Betts was 71 years old; as chairman of the board, he worked beside me, to help lead the church from a storefront to the church's current edifice. He was a staunch supporter of my community activism and advocacy. Betts was one of the first 113 African Americans to succumb to COVID-19 in Illinois. It prompted me to air my frustration on Facebook, which provided statistical information revealing that 68% of the Coronavirus cases were black. That information made Betts' death even more disheartening. Blacks being at the bottom of America's socioeconomic strata causes many to pay a steep price, often resulting in death due to the lack of access to adequate healthcare.

Healthcare however was not an issue for Betts—he was a man of means; however I can't help but wonder if there was less value placed on his life because of age or race.

In a system where blacks have been historically marginalized, oppressed and discriminated against, it's never outlandish to ask the tough questions. I insisted on the need for this to be addressed and investigated immediately! In the 21st century, this kind of racism and ageism should not exist.

As his pastor and friend, this tragedy of epic proportions truly hurt my heart. The death of Deacon Adrew Betts left a great void in the leadership helm of our church and community. He was an exemplary family man and a mentor of men.

Following the declaration of the global pandemic, cities and states began implementing various restrictions and lockdown measures within days. One of the restrictions in Illinois was to allow only a maximum of 10 people to assemble in a worship facility. It was a sight to see, and it was worse than I had imagined it would be.

When I had to lead a remnant of Deacon Bett's family into the sanctuary while reading the scripture, it nearly broke me emotionally. Seeing them all in masks, with their hands covered with gloves, socially distancing themselves from each other was heart-wrenching. It was a painful and agonizing experience that I wouldn't wish on anyone.

The atmosphere was somber and surreal, a stark reminder of the times we were living in. The traditional ways of mourning and finding solace in community were stripped away, replaced by a sense of isolation and fear. The experience underscored the profound impact of the pandemic on our communal and spiritual lives, highlighting the strength we must muster to endure such trials. The service began and hundreds tuned in to watch via live stream.

The scripture that was chosen for this eulogy was strategic and its application was most appropriate.

I wanted to use this particular subject today as we say so long to Deacon Betts, because many of us have a term of endearment that we call him. I heard some of the grandchildren call him Papa.

Terms of endearment are words that we use to express our affection for a person. Many of us are familiar with the term of endearment, baby, its a very common way we address a romantic partner. Many of us have used the word sweetheart. In the church and even in the neighborhood we may give each other a dap and say what's up "Bruh!" Well, that's also a term of endearment. Now I must admit, one of my terms of endearment. When I see one of my guys out and about, you may hear me say "Whats up Buddy!' Buddy for me, is one of my often used terms of endearment. A lot of people now use the word "Bae" in the realm of romance. You get the point!

Well at our church, Mr. Adrew Betts to a lot of us, was affectionately called DEAC! What's up Deac? Good morning Deac! It's a term of endearment. I wish I could really deal with this, but we are under strict restrictions as it relates to time and because of state lockdown measures. As we look at this term of endearment, allow me to give an attribute to describe Deacon Betts for each letter in our acronym DEAC.

The Tribute

I'm not sure that's even in the dictionary, but thats what we called him.

The **D** stands for *Dedicated*.

This was a man who was dedicated! He was unapologetically dedicated to his family. Here lies a man who truly loved his family! He raised his three children and then he was married to his wife for 46 years, until she made her transition. I told him publicly from the pulpit one Sunday. Many pastors would have possibly been afraid to make such a confession, out of fear of coming under fire for such a self-indicting admission. Being the truth teller that I am, I didn't worry about being called out or castigated, I boldly exclaimed "Deacon Betts, you are an example to all of us. Even though I am the pastor, you are the ultimate example in this church for what a man and a husband should be, because you have been dedicated to your wife until the very end of her life.

You served her, provided for her and you protected her. You took care of her, even when she was incapacitated, you were there. I am not sure if I have the maturity and make up to be so consistent and patient as you were. Don't get it confused, never in a million years would I abandon my wife during her sickness, but Deac set such a high standard and he showed us the epitome of selfless dedication as a husband. To assure that my wife would get impeccable service, I'd probably have to hire a nurse to assist me. Deac was just doing his "thang." But not only that, he then turned around and repeated the stellar service for his mom as well when her health severely deteriorated. His dedication to family makes me want to utter the words they said about Jesus in the fourth chapter of Mark, when he calmed the raging seas! What manner of man is this? Incredible and extraordinary!

He was faithful to his family, and he was faithful to his faith community, his church. Oftentimes I would call him and tell him, "Hey Deac, don't you come to church today. Please don't come today, because you've been undergoing all of these various treatments and stuff! You deserve a break today! He would always push back and say "Rev., you don't understand, I just get a lot of strength from coming to church. Then I told him, well if you must come, I'm giving you permission to come late and leave early. Yes, he was dedicated!

The next letter is **E**. Deac was *encouraging*! I have watched him over the last 25 years. I watched him mentor men, not just young men, but I've seen him be what I like to refer to as a peer mentor! That's pretty impressive when you can mentor, encourage and pour into your peers! He did that! So many men have personally told me that they are going to miss Deac, because he saw something in them that they could never see in themselves.

The next letter is A! He was affectionate! He had a loving heart! This man loved people. He really did. You know some people love crowds, but Deac loved people! He was affectionate and he loved this church. He even had it on his calendar year for 2020 to take some trips with some of the men of our church. Deacon Cobb and Deacon Sandifer y'all won't take that trip! Oh yeah, it's bittersweet today! Wherein we're going to miss him, heaven is happy! He's now resting from his labor!

The last letter is **C**! Deacon Betts was *consistent*. He was like clock-work. He was consistent. You know people can be as inconsistent as the wind; they change with the season! But He was steady! He was like a rock! He would have made 72 on his birthday. Listen, he had been with his wife for nearly 47 years! 47 years is a long time, with one wife! Now I do know some friends who can brag about being married 47 years, but they had 4 wives in the process and they end up adding all the years together cumulatively of all 4 wives. He had one wife, he was consistent!

Can you imagine me having to do a eulogy for a man of this magni-tude? He was a Christian for many years and a deacon for me for 25 years and you can add on several more years that he served with his previous pastor. Here is a person who served easily over forty some-thing years as a deacon and was a Christian fifty something years. What a testament of consistency. A whole lot of people have been Christians for 50 years, but they cannot say they only had two pastors, especially in this era of church hopping and pastoral shopping.

Some will stay here for their two years and when they get mad they move on to Reverend So and So. Then after a while they complain, "he couldn't feed me any more," so I went over to Bishop "Good and Plenty" for a little while. But, once I outgrew him, I ran across town for the hottest pastoral flavor of the month, and stayed there three years. Then I had to go get fivefold, then sevenfold, and don't forget tenfold. So now they have had ten pastors on their resume or to be printed on their obituary. No wonder some people end up being so confused and never really reach their maturity. I got a sermon I used to preach called *The Tragedy of Unfulfilled Potential*. Here is a man who was somebody special. He was Dedicated! Encouraging! Affectionate and Consistent!

The Takeaway

But more than anything he was a child of God and he let his light shine every day! That's the message we must take from his life. Let your light shine so that men may see your good work and glorify the father which art in heaven. Let's not just admire him, let's follow him, by emulating his example. Deacon Betts has taken his flight, this is just the shell that carried his body nearly 72 years.

Most of us know him for having a great interest in auto care, he took care of his cars. He valued healthcare indeed! In fact, he bragged about his health insurance. He was out there at Loyola, but he told me he was a vet, he could go to the VA and many other places. He took care of his medicare, and he utilized his dental care, but the one he valued the most was his soul care. Thats what I want to leave with someone today! Jesus asked, "What so profiteth a man to gain the whole world and lose his soul, or what shall a man give in exchange for his soul!" It's vital that you get to know Jesus for yourself!

There is no group plan, HMO, PPO, or plan on the exchange that can take the place of what God had prepared for them that love Him. Prudential does not have a rock solid enough. And Allstate's hands ain't big enough. There is no buddy pass to heaven and no friends fly free! You must have your own relationship with the King of kings. He is the one who as the Psalmist says, "Blessed *be* the Lord, *who* daily loadeth us *with benefits, even* the God of our salvation" (Psalm 68:19, KJV).

Here is the main benefit that the Lord gives to all that call on His name. Jesus said, "...I am the resurrection, and the life: he that believeth in me, though he were dead, yet shall he live" (John 11:25, KJV). Eternal life is a benefit for all who believe, that never runs out! Never fades away, and it paid in full by the blood of the Lamb! He'll never leave you or forsake you, that means He won't drop you, nor will your coverage be denied. You are secure in the Father's hand! No one can snatch you from the Father. Deac was covered by an eternal life, whole life plan signed in the blood of the Lamb, and backed by the Word of God. The same God who cannot lie, the same God that cannot fail. He is the same yesterday, today, and forever more!

The Eulogy for
Amaria Jones

But you are a chosen generation, a royal priesthood, a holy nation, His own special people, that you may proclaim the praises of Him who called you out of darkness into His marvelous light; who once were not a people but are now the people of God, who had not obtained mercy but now have obtained mercy.
I Peter 2:9-10

The Title:

Her Life Mattered

I received a call from one of my church members, a school teacher. She informed me that this family was trying to reach me to host Amaria's service. Even before considering the fact that our church's in person worship had been suspended because of the global pandemic, and that we have very limited activity, I said Yes! I knew it was the right thing to do.

The sacrifice was made, and I offered use of the church to send a clear message to everyone in this city that Her life mattered! Her life mattered regardless of the evil circumstances that ended it!

Paul put it this way, she was part of a chosen generation!

So many of us spend our entire lives trying to earn acceptance!

It's good to know even with our shortcomings and insecurities and regardless of how society labels us or stereotypes us!

Amaria was a part of A royal priesthood!

She Had direct access to God!

She was a citizen of a Holy Nation! God's own special people!

She had value because She was God's special possession!

There are two things that determine value in life: Value depends on what someone is willing to pay for something. A house, a car, a piece of art, a baseball card are only worth whatever someone is willing to pay for them. Value also depends on who has owned an item in the past. The recent auctions of Jacqueline Kennedy's and Princes Diana's personal possessions reveals that value is enhanced by previous owners.

She was called out of darkness into his marvelous light! Oh yes, her life mattered! Amaria Jones! Say her name!

Her life was taken before she even really began to live!

But let's set the record straight, she didn't do anything wrong!

She wasn't at the wrong place at the wrong time! She was at home with her family!

Her life mattered! That's why our city is grieving! Even though the vast majority of Chicagoans didn't know her.

Her life mattered, her mind mattered, her body mattered! Psalms 139:14, informs us that we were fearfully and wonderfully made. Nothing is by accident, all designed according to God's divine plan.

Amaria's soul mattered!

Her dreams mattered! Her future mattered!

The Tribute

Amaria was Ambitious!

She was able to see beyond the challenges of her own context.

I may be poor, but I am somebody!

She dreamed of becoming a lawyer!

Instead of being here to celebrate her cherished aspirations in life, now we will for many years, play the what if game!

What if she had lived? She may have become the next Barbara Jordan, Shirley Chisholm, Lori Lightfoot, the next Beyonce, J. Lo, or Michelle Obama!

What if she was the one who could have discovered the cure for cancer?

The Bible says "...the thief cometh but to steal, kill and destroy!" That's who's behind this! The hope thief that stole her life! Stealing her ambitions and stealing her dreams was a tool of the enemy! The hope thief came and took her away before she really began to live!

I'm not happy today! This event was not on our calendar!

We demand that the person who took her life be brought to justice!

We cannot allow our children to be gunned down like dogs and there be no consequences!

I believe in mercy of the court for nonviolent offenders! I don't think people should be in jail because they smoke weed sometimes! Something that "the man" has all of sudden legalized after they made billions of dollars off the incarceration of black men in these yet to be United States of America.

But read my lips, I don't advocate for the freedom of murderers! The only "no-bail" for these perpetrators is that they get *no bail!*

ILLUSTRATION

A guy in the grocery store approached me, a day after we made a plea for the community to turn in the killer of 3-year-old Mekhi! This guy came up to me with his little dirty COVID mask, that used to be white, pointing his finger! "You ought to be ashamed of yourself," he told me! On TV calling on black men to be locked up! First of all, I'm not calling for black men to be locked up!

I'm demanding that murderers be locked up whether they are black or white!

If anyone understands the state of desperation and the depths and dimension of it in our community. I do!

Decades of disinvestment!

The last mayor closed 50 schools in one year, and they were all in our neighborhood!

I'm no stranger to the strain of being black in this abysmal tale of two cities.

TIF misuse and abuse, taking tax funds that were designated for struggling and blighted communities and giving it to the affluent neighborhoods. I call it reverse Robin Hood tactics, taking what was meant for the poor and giving to the rich.

I know what it means to struggle and be black! I've been black four times. I've been a black baby, a black boy, a black man and now a black preacher!

But I'm never gonna ask for mercy for a murderer. I don't care what color he is or what neighborhood he lives in!

The Takeaway

The person who killed Amaria must not only be caught but punished to the fullest extent of the law! This madness must stop at some point!

If you are listening! Turn yourself in! You can run but you can't hide!

I'm not from the suburbs. I don't drive in! This is my neighborhood!

I know a lot of people who were in the streets! I even grew up with people who were even in gangs, and they had a street code! Whatever goes down, bad though it may be! You crossed a line when you mess with children and older people, there will be a price to pay!

You will not get away! Because God is on the throne! Jesus said in Matthew 25:40, when you have done this to the least of these, you have done it unto me!

Amaria was loved!

Her school loved her! Her community loved her! Her friends loved her! Her family loved her! That's why her grandmother rose to the occasion, put the love of Christ in her and raised her to be somebody! Her Life Mattered!

I'm glad that she believed in God and became a witness for the Lord!

Acts 1:8 tells us that every child of God is called to be a witness.

Thank God for witnesses, the world would be hopeless without witnesses!

Chicago needs witnesses to speak up! Speak up for Amaria! Speak up for the children! Speak up for our community! Speak up for the city!

So long Amaria! I'm sorry that we failed you! We should have given you a better world!

But we are here today to declare to the world that your life mattered. Your mind mattered. Your thoughts mattered. Your presence mattered. Your hopes and dreams all mattered!

You will be missed at the school!

You'll be missed at your home! You will be missed but you won't be forgotten!

Because you did nothing wrong and Jesus Christ's life shows us that there is power in the blood of the innocent! The Bible tells us that after Cain killed his brother Abel, that Abel's spilled blood cried out to God from the ground! His blood cried out for justice, just like Amaria's blood cries out for justice. As we all cry out for justice for Amaria!

ILLUSTRATION

The last thing she did was dance for her mom! On this day you had your mother's undivided attention!

But your life on earth was cut down by a gunman on the loose!

But thank God! You were a child of God! In my own mind I liken you to Miriam when the children of Israel crossed the red Sea! Once she made it over she danced!

We will see you again young queen! Until we gather on that great getting up morning dance on Hallelujah Boulevard! We love you, Amaria! Say her name. Shout her name, because certainly, her life mattered!

THE EULOGY FOR
VERNETRAS (FEFE) SINGLETON

But ye shall receive power, after that the Holy Ghost is come upon you:
and ye shall be witnesses unto me both in Jerusalem, and in all Ju-
daea, and in Samaria, and unto the uttermost part of the earth.
Acts 1:8, KJV

The Title:

A Faithful Witness

Vernetras Singleton, was affectionately known as FeFe to her family, our church and her hosts of friends. When we talk about a faithful witness, FeFe was a model to emulate, even during a taxing and grueling sickness.

For those of us who profess to be saved, Christian, or born again, may her life serve as a reminder that we are God's witnesses in this world, His and His alone!

God could have taken us instantaneously to be with him eternally, the moment we accepted Jesus Christ as our Lord and savior. Instead, he left us here for the primary purpose of sharing our faith to this lost generation.

The Acts of the Apostles, is the fifth book of the New Testament, a valuable historic presentation of the early Christian church. The book of Acts was written in Greek, presumably by St. Luke the Evangelist. The Gospel According to Luke concludes where the book of Acts begins, namely, with Christ's Ascension into heaven.

This passage highlights some very important and significant things to those who are serious about their faith.

THE NECESSITY OF THE HOLY SPIRIT

It's imperative that every believer is inhabited with the holy spirit!

You didn't have to wonder if FeFe had the Holy Spirit, if we're going to accept the telltale signs of the proof that the bible suggests.

Vs 8a says But ye shall receive power, after that the Holy Ghost is come upon you:

Being a witness is the evidence that you have it, nothing more or nothing less. It's not how high you shout! It's not how many bibles you tote or scriptures you quote! It has nothing to do with if you serve in a ministry or an auxiliary at your church, although that's a very great idea.

Having the Holy Spirit has nothing to do with weave, wigs or what you wear!

The bible declares in John 13:35, "By this shall all men know that ye are my disciples, if ye have love one another."

What good does it do to speak in tongues, and then turn around and cuss people out in English? What Good is it for you to speak in tongues during church, but won't speak to church members after church?

When you have the Holy Ghost indwelling you, the greatest evidence one can provide is the willingness and practice of being a witness! If you are claiming to be a follower of Christ and you don't habitually share your faith, at some point you must ask yourself whether or not you have the Holy Spirit or not.

As Jesus makes his exodus from the planet earth and before He returns to heaven, he explains to his disciples their assignment after his departure. That's what Acts 1:8 is all about.

The Tribute

A WITNESS TELLS WHAT THEY KNOW!

Acts 4:20, actually fleshes out the concept very beautifully. The writer expounds "For we cannot but speak the things which we have seen and heard. That almost sounds like the dictionary's definition of witness: "One who has seen or heard something and one who furnishes evidence." A witness is one who can actually say, I know beyond a shadow of a doubt, this or that to be true. As for those of us who've been born again, it's our incumbent responsibility to tell our truth about Jesus the Christ!

Those who've been healed

Those who've been made whole

Those who were headed to hell, but somebody spoke a word and shared their transformative life experience with you, It's imperative that you be a witness.

A WITNESS SHARES WHAT THEY HAVE EXPERIENCED

(Nothing more, nothing less) The concept is not about what you wandered, wished, or wanted! What you witnessed is all that matters.

A witness doesn't talk about anyone else's experience, encounters or evolution! They testify about their own experience! Our beloved sister FeFe had no problem testifying whatsoever, whether in word, work or worship! The truth is her life was a sermon! She was a "hope peddler"! Let me explain it.

How many salesmen are there in the house?

How many would consider yourself good at it?

Every good salesman knows you can't effectively sell a product that you don't believe in!

Whether it was letting her light shine on her job, sharing the love of Jesus with her fellowman, singing in the choir or sharing her faith with a stranger, it was never a problem for her because she believed in the product! She sang with so much conviction and power because she truly believed in what she sang about!

ILLUSTRATION

Can anyone remember the commercial of the Hair Club For Men back in the 1980's with Mr. Sy Sperling? This dear brother from another mother, made a fortune with his hair restoration company!

He was so effective selling millions of dollars worth of weave because he brilliantly coined the ubiquitous tagline: "I'm not just the hair club president, I'm a client!" This well groomed man would end the commercial by proceeding to hold up a photo of himself without his hair! He was saying I don't just sell the product; I use it and it works for me!

So, it is with the gospel!

If you haven't experienced Jesus, you can't effectively witness and tell a dying world that I tried the Lord and he works for me.

It's complicated to communicate Christ, when you're not a committed client!

Faithful witnesses embody the essence of Paul's proclamation in Romans 1:16. Where He boldly says "I'm not ashamed of the gospel of Jesus Christ for it is the power of God unto salvation, to everyone that believes, to the Jew first but also the Greek."

FeFe wasn't ashamed of the gospel, she wasn't ashamed of her church! This dynamic alto certainly wasn't ashamed of her choir. That's how she was so effective in bringing many to Christ and several loved ones into our faith community.

A Witness Remains Loyal To The End!

A good witness remains loyal to the end and never deviates from their original testimony! You can wake them up at 3:00 a.m. in the morning and you don't have to worry about them deviating! Their story never changes!

John the Revelator said: Revelation 2:10, the a-clause says, "be thou faithful unto death, and I will give thee a crown of life." That perfectly describes What Vernetras a.k.a. Fefe did to the end.

I visited with Fefe at Rush hospital the night before she took her fight! And she was indeed loyal to the God of her salvation, until the angels came and carried her to her heavenly home! Her thoughts were just like Paul. To be absent from the body is to be present with The Lord!

That's the picture, pattern and profile of a faithful witness!

The Takeaway

ILLUSTRATION

A prominent lawyer was being interviewed on CNN. They asked him to share a story about one of his most impressive, amazing and distinguished witnesses. He said no problem!

He recalled an instance when a blind man got robbed at gunpoint.

He mentioned how when they were in court as they were attempting to press charges against the defendant, although their fingerprints and DNA samples pointed to the man they had in court, they still had a problem because they didn't have anyone who could testify!

The judge told him, Counselor, this case would be a slam dunk if you could only produce a witness! The victimized blind man obviously could not point out the one who robbed him.

The lawyer left the courtroom and after being gone a considerable amount of time, he finally reentered the courtroom with a seeing eye dog!

At that point, they lined up several men and they marched them one by one before the dog, in the courtroom. The dog was quiet and calm throughout the entire duration, until they marched the alleged robber in front of the dog, that's when the dog went ballistic and started barking and nearly had a fit trying to attack that man! The judge hit his gavel and declared "this case is over! He's guilty as charged." So actually the lawyer's best witness ever was a dog.

Moral: What is the problem with the modern Christian who struggles in being a faithful witness? If a dog can be a witness, what about you!

When I'm asked about one of my best witnesses ever, whether it's her walk, worship or work, FeFe certainly is on my Mount Rushmore. I never shall forget that last night we were together. She said, as her years had turned into months and her months into weeks, and her weeks into days, and days into hours. "Pastor I'm going to fight to the end, but if the Lord calls me home, I've been faithful. I then prayed with her and began to exit the room and her parting words to me were "See you later!" And she's right in the words of Andrae Crouch, Soon and very soon we are going to see the King.

No more crying there.

We are going to see the King! Should there be any rivers we must cross.

Should there be any mountains we must climb, God will supply all the strength that we need give us strength till we reach the other side.

Revelation 1:5 says that Jesus is the "faithful witness." Therefore, since he is God's faithful witness, we who are born after the Spirit become Christ's faithful witnesses. And today we honor Fefe, one of Jesus's faithful witnesses!

THE EULOGY FOR
MARY WILKINS

For we know that if our earthly house of this tabernacle were dissolved, we
have a building of God, an house not made with hands, eternal in the heavens.
2 Corinthians 5:10

The Title:

It's Moving Day!

If anybody has ever had the tedious challenge of moving, you know what I am talking about! You can attest to the fact that moving is no joke.

It is a time of stress and hurry. Time always goes by fast when it is time to move. Not only is moving day stressful and annoying. Moving day can be a sad day, because you are leaving the familiar.

You leave behind old friends and acquaintances. You leave the old neighborhood. You›re just left with memories of what your life used to be like.

Somebody say Moving day!

The truck has pulled up to the house ready to go!

It is ready to be loaded up with your belongings ready to move from a place that you once cherished. A place you once called home!

It is Moving day.

Regardless of all the anxieties and jitters that naturally accompany moving, moving can also be a blessing and is a blessing, when you're moving on to greater things.

When you move there is pain in the separation, but also there will be immense joy that comes with the new place that you are now going to be a resident of. You are moving from the old to the new, a new community. You are transitioning into new horizons, a place of new hopes and dreams. This very fact is true for the believers who have all experienced a big move in their life. You moved from darkness into light. You moved from a place of unrest and confusion into a place of peace. You moved from a life of sin to a life that is saved.

The Tribute

Sister Mary Wilkins left this house that she lived in for more than seven decades but she's not homeless! Her business was fixed a long time ago in Pickens Alabama.

There's a great reward in store for her faithful and fiery service. In fact, Sister Mary Wilkins was such a humble, God-fearing woman that if she had a say this morning, I have no doubt she would be insistent, adamant, and emphatic that I don't preach about her but tell the folks about Jesus. That's the humble soul she was. Her life was a shining example of faith, trust, hope, and love.

Sister Mary Wilkins dedicated herself to serving her God through serving others with a fervent spirit and a loving heart. She lived her life not for recognition, but for the glory of God, always pointing others toward His grace and mercy. She shunned the spotlight. Her unwavering faith was evident in every action, every word, and every gesture of kindness she extended to those around her.

I never knew her to have a lot of money, but she was rich, in fact very rich in faith! She truly believed that God was still in the prayer answering business!

I could hear her saying "Preach about Jesus! Preach to the Living." I get the point, because we all preach our own funerals by the life we live. She lived a great life for Christ. She has a great mansion in store for her because of that.

IT'S A PERFECT PLACE: The bible says "it's a Building of God."

God made it, so its perfect!

Things in this world are feeble, flawed and fraudulent.

That's why you can't get too caught up on the cash clothes and creature comforts of this world!

IT'S A PERMANENT PLACE: Paul said it's eternal in the heavens.

He uses the imagery of a tent to describe the human body.

Paul was a tent maker by profession so it's not a surprise that he uses the terminology of his profession and language that his listeners would clearly understand and grasp.

It's a portable home for nomadic people.

You don't build a permanent residence if you're just passing through!

Ms. Mary knew that she didn't come here to stay and that she was just passing through this world, and she lived that way as a faithful steward of Jesus Christ.

She understood that life on earth was temporary, and she approached each day with a sense of purpose and devotion. Her humble spirit reflected her deep faith and commitment to serving God. Ms. Mary never sought earthly accolades or personal praise! Instead of pursuing material wealth she invested her time and energy in things of eternal value! She taught us all that only what you do for Christ will last.

TIME IN CHURCH

She loved and supported her church and spent time serving in the choir.

INVESTMENT IN CHILDREN

She Invested her time and her children and grandchildren. She was a single parent but it never distracted or deterred her from raising 3 responsible God fearing children.

She was a prayer warrior and a pastoral intercessor!

Every Pastor values having wise elders within their congregation who see their assignment as a calling to pray for the pastor and his family.

SHE WAS A PRAISER!

Mary was a praiser! The Bible says that God inhabits the praises of His people. Mary's energy, excitement, and emotions during our services reflected her deep desire to make that happen.

Mary's worship was vibrant and heartfelt, a true expression of her love and devotion to our God. Her praise was not an outward show but a genuine external reflection of her inner faith and joy.

She understood the power of praise in bringing God's presence into our midst, and she dedicated herself to creating an atmosphere where His spirit could dwell. When she was at church, you were assured of having a power packed service.

Her enthusiasm was contagious and oftentimes would light a fire under the deadheads and inspire them to join us in heartfelt worship.

SHE GAVE HER TREASURE

As a member, she was low maintenance. She didn't require the church to hold her hand or to pamper her whenever she had a health scare or a medical challenge! Oftentimes she would be missing from her place in the choir a few Sundays, and I'd see her and inquire about her whereabouts, and she would say I was in the hospital, but I didn't want to bother you Pastor. You have so much on your plate.

The Takeaway

III. PRECIOUS PLACE

Sister Mary has moved to a perfect place, a permanent place and finally a precious place.

We can classify it as a precious place because we will be in the presence of The Lord.

Vs.8 "We are confident, I say, and willing rather to be absent from the body, and to be present with the Lord.

We can list all the amenities that the Scripture tell us about heaven.

Streets paved with gold. Pearly gates. Trees good for the healing of the nations, and many mansions over there! But at the end of the day, it's being in the presence of Jesus that makes heaven heavenly. Not even He can make something that's better than Him!

We will miss her dearly, and the world feels a lot colder without her presence. Family don't torment yourselves by replaying the transition of Ms. Mary in your mind. She has moved into her new, heavenly home.

While her absence leaves an enormous void, we can find comfort in knowing that she is now in a place of eternal peace and she's resting comfortably with the Lord, where there is no more pain, sorrow, or suffering.

May the Lord give us the spirit to celebrate the beautiful soul she was and the eternal home she has now entered.

I'm reminded of an old lady who used to catch the evening bus every day at 5:00pm and would get off right in front of the cemetery. One day a few little boys decided to find out what this old woman was doing and where she was going. So, they secretly followed her! They ducked and dodged and hid behind tomb stones and trees as they followed her through the cemetery.

They followed her only to discover that she wasn't living in the cemetery after all! To their dismay, she wasn't crazy, not one bit, she was just passing through the cemetery. She had a beautiful home on the other side of the cemetery. Don't be so paranoid by the cemetery that you forget what God has promised you on the other side of the cemetery. In case you missed it, Mary Wilkins will not be staying at the cemetery. Her new home is on the other side!

"Servant of God! Well done! Rest from thy loved employ! The battle fought, the victory won, Enter thy master's joy."

THE EULOGY FOR
DOROTHY LOVE

David mustered the men who were with him and appointed over them com-
manders of thousands and commanders of hundreds. David sent out his troops,
a third under the command of Joab, a third under Joab's brother Abishai son of
Zeruiah, and a third under Ittai the Gittite. The king told the troops, "I my-
self will surely march out with you." But the men said, "You must not go out;
if we are forced to flee, they won't care about us. Even if half of us die, they
won't care; but you are worth ten thousand of us.[a] It would be better now for
you to give us support from the city"
II Samuel 18: 1-4

The Title:

Irreplaceable

Sunday was a bittersweet day for me as pastor of Greater St John Bible Church. On the day that Dorothy passed, back in August of 2014, 13 new members joined church. It was a bittersweet day for our church, on this particular Sunday the Lord blessed our evangelistic efforts significantly, yet on the same day he took from us a woman whose value was more than twenty church members. Oh, what an emotional and spiritual roller coaster ride it was. What a remarkable juxtaposition.

The historic backdrop to this text is critical because it reveals another juxtaposition. Absalom is attempting a massive *coup de tat* on his father King David! Imagine that, of all the people to turn on you, it's the child you loved so much! As they prepared for Absalom's attack,

David's men insisted that he not join them on the battlefield (vs 4). Their reasoning was clear: David was too valuable and, quite frankly, irreplaceable. They wanted to continue to benefit from his impeccable wisdom and unparalleled leadership skills. In their estimation, losing any other leader or even thousands of soldiers was bearable, but losing King David was not an option. His power, presence, and personality were truly irreplaceable.

These men recognized that David's contributions went beyond his physical prowess. His strategic mind, his ability to inspire, and his unwavering faith were essential to their cause. David's absence on the battlefield was a testament to his unmatched importance; his leadership from afar was deemed more crucial than his sword in hand. They knew that his very essence provided strength and confidence to his people, and that his guidance was the cornerstone of their potential victory.

The Tribute

In the same way, we gather here between these sacred walls to remember and honor the irreplaceable spirit of the compassionate and selfless Sister Dorothy Love. Like King David, Dorothy's presence in our lives was a source of wisdom, strength, and unwavering support. She touched the hearts of everyone she encountered, leaving an indelible mark that will never fade. Her legacy of love, kindness, and resilience will continue to inspire us, just as David's legacy inspired his people. Today, we celebrate Dorothy's extraordinary life and the profound impact she had on us, her family, church and community. Let's compare the attributes of Queen Dorothy and King David.

A SKILLFUL COORDINATOR

David was a skillful coordinator. From this text, it is evident that he masterfully organized his army into three divisions and strategically appointed captains to lead each unit. His ability to delegate authority and structure his forces with such precision demonstrates his exceptional leadership and organizational skills. David's keen insight into the strengths and capabilities of his men allowed him to optimize their effectiveness in battle, ensuring that each division operated cohesively and efficiently. This meticulous planning and strategic foresight were crucial to the success and resilience of his army. A trait that David shared with Sister Dorothy Love! She did that almost second nature! She was a meticulous planner. She wasn't a let the chips fall where they may person. No, she wanted those chips to fall a certain way.

FAMILY

In her family she was the leader and was well respected for empowering other family members and making them feel important and like they mattered!

FRIENDS

Dorothy was respected as a skillful coordinator among her various circle of friends. Her ability to bring people together and organize events with ease was admired, adored and appreciated by all who knew her. Dorothy's keen sense of detail and her talent for managing various tasks ensured that every gathering she arranged was a standout success. D Love took care of business! Whether planning community events, coordinating social gatherings, or offering support to those in need. She got things done!

FAITH COMMUNITY

What I like about Dorothy the most is the fact that she used her creative competence, strategic savvy and practical proficiency for the joy, the jubilation and for her journey for Jesus! I never shall forget how she was supposed to help me organize my mom's 60th birthday party and instead of following my lead, she took the bull by the horns and single handedly coordinated it by herself. I also remember when I launched our church's scholarship efforts and initiatives back in 2001, Dorothy was one of the first church leaders who bought in and worked to lay the foundation for this effort. It's all because she saw the vision, as well as the value and virtue in our young people.

A SENSE OF COMPASSION

Real leaders are compassionate! David displayed love even when his son tried to usurp his authority!

Dorothy displayed unconditional love even when her strong hand of discipline was rejected by some! She loved anyhow, that applies to family and friends!

MOTHERLY

She was motherly by nature, and that's why she could check you without causing offense. As a maternal figure to many, her words carried weight because you always knew she loved you and had your best interest at heart! Her ability to blend firmness with love earned her respect and admiration, making her a pillar of strength and guidance at Greater St John Church.

MENTOR

Her willingness to activate her mentorship prowess is what made her so extremely valuable around here! She trained and inspired a plethora of leaders. She was a mediator! She was a keeper of the peace! I can't help but wonder "Who's gonna keep y'all from killing each other, now that Dorothy is gone! She was like E.F. Hutton. Remember, the old EF Hutton commercial that said, when E.F. Hutton speaks people listen. Well when Dorothy spoke, people listened. To get people to stop arguing and listen today is a valuable gift!

STRENGTH OF CHARACTER

Another reason she's irreplaceable is her Strength of Character A. She was fun! Dorothy was one of the most devout and serious-minded Christians I have ever met, but she wasn't a pseudo-saint who was so heavenly-minded that she was no earthly good. Her conviction was that believers needed balance in their lives. After church, she would always welcome friends, family, and fellow church members into her home. Dorothy believed that living a faithful life didn't mean sacrificing joy and camaraderie. Her home was a place of warmth and laughter, where spiritual discussions mingled with everyday conversations. She believed people could be themselves and enjoy the simple pleasures of life.

B. She was a finisher. If she was given an assignment, or if she just took charge of one. You could count on her completing the task. She Wasn't a spiritual baby wherein you had to hold her hand until completion of the task.

C. She was friendly. Proverbs 18:24 says, "A man that hath friends must shew himself friendly: and there is a friend that sticketh closer than a brother. Dorothy embodied friendship! She has a way of making us all feel special.

D. She was faithful to the end! Some folks will use anything as an excuse to stop fulfilling their obligations. Excuses like, my ear aches. My eyes are running! My nose is sniffling! I don't feel good! No not Dorothy!

The Takeaway

She clearly took Revelation 2:10 seriously, where John the revelator pens these words: "Fear none of those things which thou shalt suffer: behold, the devil shall cast some of you into prison, that ye may be tried; and ye shall have tribulation ten days: be thou faithful unto death, and I will give thee a crown of life."

I asked her daughter Vanessa to give me a word to describe her mother, and She said strong! What a perfect description I believe it was the power of the Holy Spirit that enabled her to exhibit so much strength on a number of fronts in the midst of her own challenges that she encountered on this journey called life.

ILLUSTRATION

This makes me think of my comic book superheroes, they all were strong. But they would all get in trouble sometimes! I remember on one occasion when superman was in trouble and it looked like he was losing the battle! He was my guy, and I couldn't bear knowing that he was getting an excessive beat down from Lex Luther. So, I got impatient and turned to the end of the book to see how things turned out! And When I got to the end, I was pleasantly surprised that Superman made a comeback and was victorious over his nemesis.

Sometimes in life when I'm at my lowest point and can't see my way! And I wonder how things will turn out. So, once again, I turned to the end of the book, to Revelation 21:1-4. But I insert myself, as I take my ecstatic flight through the text where it says:

Then I saw a new heaven and a new earth, for the first heaven and the first earth had passed away, and there was no longer any sea. I saw the

Holy City, the new Jerusalem, coming down out of heaven from God, prepared as a bride beautifully dressed for her husband. And I heard a loud voice from the throne saying, "Look! God's dwelling place is now among the people, and he will dwell with them. They will be his people, and God himself will be with them and be their God. 'He will wipe every tear from their eyes.

There will be no more death! No more mourning or crying! No more pain! For the old order of things has passed away." Who's going to be there? A crowd of 144,000 all from the tribes of Israel. But then I saw another really big group, a crowd that no man can number. Then one of the elders asked me, "Do you know who these people are that are dressed in these white robes? Do you know where they come from?" "Sir," I answered, "you must know."

Then he told me: "These are the ones who have gone through the great suffering. They have washed their robes in the blood of the Lamb and have made them white. And so they stand before the throne of God and worship him in his temple day and night. They have the victory! They have access! They have heaven's best!

That's the crowd that Dorothy will be in! That's the crowd that I will be in! That's the crowd that will include all of us who loved the Lord and let our joy be known while we tabernacled down here on these mundane shores. All of us irreplaceable people, will end up in an irreplaceable place called the new heaven and the new earth wherein righteousness dwells forever, and ever!

The Eulogy for
Louis Lee

*But Stephen, full of the Holy Spirit, looked up to heaven and saw
the glory of God, and Jesus standing at the right hand of God.
"Look," he said, "I see heaven open and the Son of Man standing
at the right hand of God."*
Acts 7:55-56

The Title:

The Man For Whom Jesus Stood!

This Is the only time recorded in the scripture that Jesus stood up in heaven! That's a big deal! There had to be something very special about the service, sacrifice and selflessness of this man.

Who is this Stephen personality you may ask, that prompted the Lord to stand up for, and how is this relevant to the life of Deacon Louis Lee! What stands out about the protagonist of our text that the pastor contrasts him with our honored friend, family leader and faithful Christian servant?

Stephen was one of the seven original deacons of the new testament church. He was a deacon for real, not just one in title or in name alone! He was involved! He was engaged and he was faithful to the work of the kingdom!

Stephen has a vision of the Lord Standing, not sitting at the right hand of God, but standing.

All seven names of the original deacons are listed in Acts 6:5, This proposal pleased the whole group. They chose Stephen, a man full of faith and of the Holy Spirit; also Philip, Procorus, Nicanor, Timon,

Parmenas, and Nicolas from Antioch, a convert to Judaism (NIV).

The two standout deacons were Stephen and Phillip.

Well Greater St John has had two standout deacons for a significant season also! The attributes of Stephen are mentioned and they are very similar ironically to our most esteemed Deacon Lee.

The Tribute

HIS ROLE

He served. A deacon is a servant. We learn from the life of Stephen that God honors faithfulness.

Louis Lee rendered exemplary service as a deacon. He was on my board, and he had my back!

Down through the years he took some major hits for having my back! It carries a lot of weight and provides a great deal of validation when a strong established man of stature serves on your board. Some people are in your cabinet but not in your corner! Thank God for Lee having the spirit of Deacon Stephen.

Just like Stephen, Deacon Lee pointed everyone to Jesus. I can think of many people who either came to Christ or who joined the church because of his invitation.

Deacon Lee was instrumental in leading Julia Briscoe to our church. She then was instrumental in bringing her family. The great singer Ms. Erica Stevenson and her sister Peaches all came because of him. Pat Hood who has been here is also a proverbial fish that Deacon Lee caught for the Lord. I will never forget how he was instrumental in leading the late Nick Charles Norris to Christ.

This stands out because I had the honor of baptizing Brother Charles at the age of 66.

LEE, LIKE STEPHEN, WAS FULL OF THE HOLY SPIRIT!

I learned a long time ago that you don't judge a person's degree of Godliness by how loud they shout! It wasn't because of any Pentecostal proclivities but it was evidenced by his soul winning and his love for humanity.

HE WAS DEPENDABLE!

The membership, both young and old, could depend on this gentleman, the pride and joy of Glendora Mississippi. His friends, faith community and his family could depend on him. He was a father figure for many of his nieces and nephews, and for several young people who attended our church.

He wasn't the kind of leader that was just with you in spirit! (You gotta watch out for people, who are just with you in spirit!)

Although it's great to have well-wishers, you need someone to get in the trenches with you! If I ever had to be in a foxhole with anyone, it would be Lee, because we've been in foxholes and he has an impeccable track record.

He loved the church! He loved the community! He loved Christ and His creator and, he never saw any tension in loving church and pastor simultaneously!

ILLUSTRATION

When Deacon Lee joined our church, I was 27 years old and he was 47. You will never know how much of a source of encouragement he was to me. I'm glad that I had the opportunity to thank him for his decades of service, sacrifice and selflessness to our church and for his solidarity with me!

He had a way with words, he once told me 'You don't have to ever worry about me shooting a hole in the boat that I'm riding in! I later discovered that he meant to convey to me how foolish it is for people to attempt to destroy something that they are a part of.

Stephen was the church's first martyr!

That's how much he loved the church and was committed to it, so much that he gave his life for it. In a real sense Deacon Lee was a martyr for Christ! He gave his life to the church, his clan, his community and to Christ.

He will be missed! Some people will pass away and you will feel sad, you may even go into shock, depending on how they passed. It stings because they were nice people or because you know there will be a void in their family and community, but you can't really say that you will miss them, because they were absent more than they were present. That's not the case with this dear brother! Lee will be missed!

Missed at church outings! Missed at speaking engagements!

Missed by college students who come home for the summer!

Missed by those he loaned money to! He's really gonna be missed by the people who still owe him!

Missed at the monthly family dinner!

He was old school. He often shared with me how each month his family would gather to dine and fellowship. He took great pride in that, and it's something that I deeply admired. He will be missed at the family reunion! He would not miss those. He's already missed at Greater St John Bible Church. His absence leaves a great void, and I can't help but wonder who will step up. I'm not worried, I'm certain someone will, because Lee set a great example and he didn't mind mentoring and sharing his wisdom.

ILLUSTRATION

I don't know if many of you are familiar with the Hammond B3. The Hammond B3 organ is an electric organ, invented by Laurens Hammond and John M. Hanert and first manufactured in 1935. Various models have been produced, most of which use sliding drawbars to create a variety of sounds. This organ has become famous in churches as a cheaper alternative to pipe organs! The sound was so good that no one wanted pipe organs anymore. The last Hammond B3 organ was made in 1973 shortly after Mr. Laurens Hammond died! Well believe it or not they are offering $10,000 for the Hammond B3. In times like these we could use that around here in a variety of ways. But the truth is that it would be foolish to say goodbye to that masterpiece, because they don't make them like that anymore!

So it is, with Deacon Lee, his family, his friends and certainly his church will miss him greatly because they don't make men like him anymore.

His Rhetoric!

His words! Stephen knew the Book and was a profound orator! Stephen delivered a dynamic sermon in Acts 6.

Lee wasn't a teacher *per se* of the word, but he was a lifelong student of the Word and oh did he love the Word. You could expect him in Sunday School and bible class like clockwork.

His Wisdom!

The word was reflected in his wisdom! Nod your head if he ever gave you some invaluable wisdom! Let me nod first, because he spoke life into me!

His Rewards!

Just Like Stephen, so was Deacon Lee! He stood up for Jesus and Jesus stood up for him! He Stood in solidarity with Stephen!

He Stood in Support. All the way from the cotton patches of Mississippi!

He gave him a standing ovation! "Well Done thy good and faithful servant!"

They thought when they stoned Stephen, he was a victim! Not true. He was a victor!

Let me quote the words of Apostle Paul for those of you who have the tendency to have selective amnesia! To live is Christ and to die is gain.

ILLUSTRATION

I talked with Reverend James Austin, another soldier that served here, before he went back to live in Mississippi, the other day and he shared with me his last conversation with Deacon Lee. He asked him like only Reverend Austin could. "How you feel?" Instead of that energetic and vibrant response, in a very sober manner he stated "Cancer got me!" Austin told me that he rebuked the statement and said Naw! Jesus got you! Jesus got you! I know He's got you, because I've been with you a long time! And I've seen Him in you!

There is another alternative! Satan could have you, but Jesus got you!

He's right! He's no longer here! That's not his body that lies in front of us, that's just the body that housed him for 77 years.

𝕿𝖍𝖊 𝕿𝖆𝖐𝖊𝖆𝖜𝖆𝖞!

As we say so long to our friend, I'm reminded of the annual race held in Austin. Every September we have the Austin Power 5K! It's a 5k race in the Austin community! I've supported it many years, but it's very humbling! Because there are so many much better, agile, and quicker runners than me! So many who start off with me pass me by! The last year I ran. I almost quit because of that frustration, but I kept on pushing! Knees were sore, wind was short! Discouraged! But I kept pushing! Sweating profusely! The best part about the race however is the reception you get when you finish the race! People who finished the race before me, were welcoming me home! The other day Deacon Lee completed his race! I can see loved ones waiting at heaven's gate! Loved ones will be waiting to welcome him home. His parents will be waiting, he has a brother who will be welcoming him home! Some church members and fellow deacons will be waiting but most of all King Jesus will be there Saying welcome home! Well done, thou good and faithful servant. Rest from your love employed!

By this time, I was too emotional and couldn't go any longer. My final words as I put my hand on the casket were "Rest, Rest, Rest."

THE EULOGY FOR
SISTER ROBBIE REYNOLDS

And being in Bethany in the house of Simon the leper, as he sat at meat, there came a woman having an alabaster box of ointment of spikenard very precious; and she brake the box, and poured it on his head. And there were some that had indignation within themselves, and said, Why was this waste of the ointment made? For it might have been sold for more than three hundred pence, and have been given to the poor. And they murmured against her. And Jesus said, Let her alone; why trouble ye her? she hath wrought a good work on me. For ye have the poor with you always, and whensoever ye will ye may do them good: but me ye have not always. She hath done what she could: she is come aforehand to anoint my body to the burying. Verily I say unto you, Wheresoever this gospel shall be preached throughout the whole world, this also that she hath done shall be spoken of for a memorial of her.
Mark 14:3-9, KJV

The Title:
She Did What She Could!

We are here to celebrate the life of a beautiful Soul! You and I have something to be grateful for! A special celebration was taking place at the home of Simon the leper! They were celebrating his miraculous healing. Among his guests were Mary, Martha, Lazarus and Jesus. In this text we see a woman who did all she could for her savior! That was Sister Robbie Reynolds for sure.

WE SEE A PROLIFIC ACT

The perfume used on Jesus' feet was very expensive!

Some of Jesus' trusted disciples called it a waste!

From their perspective she should have sold it and given the proceeds to the Jerusalem Red Cross or to Israel's Salvation Army.

But for Mary her unexpected ritualistic engagement was a generous expression of extravagant love.

Sister Robbie Reynolds, whose remains lie here today, was very similar! Don't miss the point—she didn't have the material wealth that others might have had, but oh, was she rich!

Robbie's richness can't be measured in dollars and cents, but in the depth of her character, the warmth of her spirit, and the love she shared with everyone around her. Her wealth was evident in her kindness, her generosity, and her unwavering faith.

She was generous with what she had!

She was generous with her: love, time and resources

ILLUSTRATION

God knows how you feel! A story is told of a great woman of faith who had a child late in life. She did everything right. She went to school, earned degrees, and worked a few years to build her financial empire. She was a committed Christian and a devout, supportive member of her church. Fate had it that she married a wonderful Christian man, and they later had a child together. What a beautiful family it was!

One day however, tragedy struck. While she was out walking with her baby in his stroller, an out-of-control car drove up on the sidewalk and killed their only child. This was a devastating blow for both of them. The mother had such difficulty coping that, even after counseling and many prayers, she still couldn't manage. She eventually left home, quit her job, and refused to return to her church.

After being gone for several months, she stumbled upon her pastor at the local mall. Although she tried to run in the other direction, he tracked her down and tried to minister to her and offer his support. He asked about her and how the church could help. She reluctantly declined his overture. She eventually asked the question of the ages: "Pastor, I have one question that I need you to answer for me. Where was God when my baby got killed?"

The pastor paused for a few seconds and then replied, "He was in the same place that He was when His Son took nails in His hands, rivets in His feet, and a spear in His side." He knows how you feel!

Family Please know that God knows how you feel today, but most of all, in spite of everything that's going on, He's still on the throne.

A PROVIDENTIAL ACT

When they criticized Mary for wasting the money instead of using it to feed the poor!

Jesus responds by saying "the poor you shall have with you always! But I won't be with you always!"

Sister Reynolds, knew that only what you do for Christ will last!

Before her health failed her, she served with all of her heart and gave to the kingdom everything that she had. She was dedicated and committed to her faith.

Her devotion was evident in every aspect of her life. She volunteered tirelessly, whether it was ushering in the early days or helping the mission with special projects.

Sister Reynolds lived a meaningful life and did something with her dash!

The bible constantly reminds us of the brevity and uncertainty of life. "You do not even know what will happen tomorrow. What is your life? You are a mist that appears for a little while and then vanishes" (James 4:14).

The Tribute

A PRACTICAL ACT

Mary did all she could. We readily see this kind gesture as a practical act (Mark 14:8). For her, there was no time to go to the market, to prepare a meal, or to weave a robe. She leaves that to Martha or others and decides to use what she had.

Sister Reynolds did the same, she used what she had.

I witnessed many years of her kindness. She had a loving heart!

Love is as love does!

She spoiled her children.

I remember one time she came to church with her bonus son, the 17-year-old, when he was real young. I made the mistake of calling him her grandson. And boy did she snap! She let me have it! I'm not the grandmama she hollered, I'm the mama! Who's feeding him, she added.

A PERCEPTIVE ACTION

Jesus had often spoken of his death. He mentioned at least seventeen times that he would die and be resurrected. But his followers didn't get the picture. Sometimes the truth nearest us is the truth that evades us. Their spiritual ears didn't hear, but Mary's did.

Mary knew that a person who died as a criminal—according to the law of that day—was denied the customary anointing oils and perfumes. This act shows that now only does Mary display her love, but she also displays her spiritual perception. Jesus would die, but not unsaluted! She was thoughtful! We have to be grateful for the thoughtful people who God's grace places in our path!

As a pastor, I thank God for long distance runners. Many come and go, some are here for a reason and some for a season. She was a long-distance runner letting her light shine for the glory of God. Certainly!

If you can think of a time, she ever called to check on you, tell the Lord thank you! When you were going through a tough period in your life, if she ever encouraged you, remember her kindness. If you ever ran into her and she greeted you with a kind word or a humorous thought, put your hands together in appreciation! If you ever ate her cooking, you know it was a blessing. If she ever gave you anything, whether a gift or some money, know you're not alone in your gratitude. She did what she could, and that's all God is asking of us. Give your best!

The Takeaway

Sister Reynolds loved my family! She had a special affection for my children. She knew them all their lives. As we celebrate Sister Reynolds, I can't help but think of my kids when they were young, and we lived on the 1500 block of Waller Ave. When they were small, we would watch games on our TV in the basement of our home. On a number of occasions, I remember they would fall asleep during the game. Marcus was bigger, so I would wake him up and walk him to his bed, but Nicole—I would just pick her up and carry her to her room.

I will never forget overhearing a conversation between them one Saturday. Nicole said, "I must be sleepwalking because last night I remember being downstairs, and now this morning, I'm upstairs." Marcus pushed back and said, "Cut it out! You weren't sleepwalking! You fell asleep downstairs, and Daddy picked you up and put you in his arms and carried you upstairs." Well, that's what happened to this precious soul. The other day, Sister Reynolds fell asleep downstairs and woke up upstairs! Upstairs! In a city where the wicked shall cease from troubling and the weary shall be at rest. Upstairs where every day will be Sunday, every month the month of May, and every year the year of Jubilee. Upstairs in that new Jerusalem! I look forward to that beautiful day. Oh, they tell me of a home far beyond the skies, Oh, they tell me of a home far away! Oh, they tell me of a home where no storm clouds rise! Oh, they tell me of an uncloudy day. Enter into God's rest Sister Reynolds. Some people never did what they could do. Others got by on what they must do, but sister Reynolds did what she could do.

THE EULOGY FOR
MOTHER ANGELEAN STOCKDALE

Who can find a virtuous woman? for her price is far above rubies. The heart of her husband doth safely trust in her, so that he shall have no need of spoil. She will do him good and not evil all the days of her life. She maketh herself coverings of tapestry; her clothing is silk and purple. She openeth her mouth with wisdom; and in her tongue is the law of kindness. She looketh well to the ways of her household, and eateth not the bread of idleness. Her children arise up, and call her blessed; her husband also, and he praiseth her.
Proverbs 31:10-12,22;27-28

The Title:

The Profile of a Godly Woman

Many years ago, my wife and I visited New Orleans for a vacation. At that time, we visited a restaurant called the Ruby Slipper. It was buzzing! Everyone urged us to check out this 5-star cafe. It was located at 2nd and Magazine. We walked to the restaurant from our hotel and had a big problem finding it. We walked back and forth on Magazine Street. Unbeknownst to us, it was right under our nose! It wasn't until however we ran into a man with a white jacket on and chef's hat that we realized how close we were to the establishment. And we inquired from him. We were right in front of the building, but we didn't see it because the building was far from the sidewalk and was in the yard. How did we manage to miss this masterpiece and we were standing right in front of it? That's life, sometimes we're so close to greatness that we don't recognize it! I submit to you today that the same principle is true with one who has been among us, Mother Angelean Stockdale! For all these years you've been so close to greatness and you didn't recognize it! Solomon in describing this virtuous woman gives the profile of a Godly woman who in many ways mirrors the life of a Mother Stockdale, one of the founding members of our church.

She was special! Solomon said her price is far above rubies.

Can we thank God for her love! Can we thank God for her wisdom! And most of all thank God for her prayers! This virtuous woman's contribution was a plethora of prayers for this congregation. It was crucial and vital in the church's early and our most vulnerable season.

The Tribute

SHE WAS DEVOTED TO HER FAMILY

Verse 27 states, She looketh well to the ways of her household, and eateth not the bread of idleness. Mother Stockdale loved her family, both her immediate and extended family.

Three of her older cousins attended our church for years and she always talked fondly about them. She called them Vicky and Minnie Lee, and Brother Aubrey Moses.

She and her late husband raised their children with love and dedication. When I first arrived here as a young pastor, they graciously hosted me at their house and often shared stories about her family. She spoke fondly of how he had encouraged her to leave her job so that she could be at home with their children every day.

The two of them took great pride in their teamwork, with him as the breadwinner and her as the homemaker. Their partnership was a testament to their commitment to family and to each other. They created a nurturing and stable home environment, where their children could thrive.

When her granddaughter Velinda was born, because of their advanced age, people advised them against becoming the guardians, but they defied popular opinion and took their grandchild in and raised her like their own.

And I'm so glad that she did!

I met her nearly 35 years ago, and she was taking care of people then. She took care of her mother, and later she took care of her husband.

SHE DEMONSTRATED HER FAITH

Matthew 5:16 admonishes us to: "Let your light so shine before men, that they may see your good works, and glorify your Father which is in heaven."

SHE HONORED HER PASTOR!

One of the ways she demonstrated her faith was in the manner she honored and revered her pastor. In fact, she had a healthy love for all pastors. Through the good, bad and ugly, she honored her pastor. She honored me and every other pastor that preceded me!

I remember her in my early days as pastor of this church assuring me that this church needed a pastor. She said "I love the deacons! They are some good men, but God calls pastors to shepherd his flock, and I know God sent you here because we prayed for you."

She was quite aware of Hebrews 13:17,

> Obey them that have the rule over you, and submit yourselves: for they watch for your souls, as they that must give account, that they may do it with joy, and not with grief: for that is unprofitable for you.

SHE TRUSTED THE WORD OF GOD AND REVERENCED THE SAVIOR!

She Demonstrated her faith, She honored her pastor, She trusted the word of God and She reverenced The Savior!

Proverbs 31:30 states, "Favour is deceitful, and beauty is vain: but a woman that feareth the LORD, she shall be praised."

Mother is in heaven today, a prepared place for prepared people.

She has reached the place that her amazing faith and devotion always pointed towards. Heaven, a realm of eternal peace and joy, is reserved for those who have lived their lives in readiness for this divine transition.

Many have come to support the family today, some have come to honor her memory and to celebrate a great life. But as we look in the casket for the viewing, in actuality This is not Mother Stockdale! This is not your mom or grandmother!

The Takeaway

A lot of us have said some wonderful things about her today! She left a lasting legacy! And she was a good steward! She did her part with family, friends and faith community.

She went the extra mile in the early days to keep this church's doors open. The Stockdale's family was one of the families who sacrificed significantly to pay bills. Well, She's in heaven now, but it's not because of her goodness. She was a very good woman, but no one is good enough to earn a place in heaven!

She's in heaven now because she trusted Christ and the cross of Calvary! While she won't be able to attend the next family reunion y'all plan, I'm so glad that a long time ago down in the state of Missouri she registered for the greatest reunion of all time. She went to a meeting one night, and her heart wasn't right, and something got a hold of her!

Indeed, there is a greater reunion that she's headed to, one far beyond our earthly gatherings. She is now in the presence of the Lord, partaking in the eternal reunion with all the saints who have gone before her. This heavenly reunion is a place of everlasting joy! This heavenly reunion is a place of eternal peace. This heavenly reunion is where there are no goodbyes, only eternal fellowship with our Savior and loved ones.

Mother's faith in Christ secured her place in this divine gathering, and while we will miss her at our family reunions, we can take comfort in knowing that she is celebrating in the greatest reunion ever. Her life and faith remind us to prepare ourselves for that same glorious day, where we will be reunited in heaven, forever in the presence of God!

When you get there tell brother Stockdale, that I'm on my way! Tell Mother Allen, Mother Wilbourn, Gladys Young, Brother Aubrey Moses and your children just a few more days of the rising and setting of the suns! When I can read my title clear, to mansions in the sky! I'll bid farewell to all of my friends, knowing that God will wipe away my tears! Some glad morning, when this life is over. I'm going to fly away and be at rest! "When I die, Hallelujah by and by, I'll fly away!" So long Mother Stockdale, sit down servant, sit down! Sit down and rest a little while.

The Eulogy for
Sister Tracey Showers

His lord said unto him, Well done, thou good and faithful servant: thou hast been faithful over a few things, I will make thee ruler over many things: enter thou into the joy of thy lord.
Matthew 25:21

The Title:

A Faithful Servant

Sister Tracey Showers, was a dedicated young woman of our church who served in three vital areas: the missionary ministry, as a praise dance leader, and in the media ministry. Tragically, she was gunned down on election night 2023 in front of her home, just after picking up her daughter from work. This egregious act has left our church community rattled and deeply emotional. As I begin speaking, my mind is racing, and I am struggling to conceal my emotions.

I am not happy today! I'm hurting for this family! I'm hurting for our church! I'm especially hurting for our city! Whoever the monster is that's still on the loose, you took the life of someone who would give you her heart, if she thought she could live without it!

Gun violence is completely out of control! Far too many innocent people are losing their lives to this madness in Chicago. This horrific tragedy happened on election night! Which highlights and magnifies the urgency of dealing with this evil epidemic. Crimes don't get solved in Chicago, so killers are emboldened!

The Tribute

In the midst of our pain and tears, spiritually we know this is not the end. Tracey was God's Faithful servant!

John the revelator said "And I heard a voice from heaven saying unto me, Write, Blessed are the dead which die in the Lord from henceforth: Yea, saith the Spirit, that they may rest from their labors; and their works do follow them.'

The apostle said "But I would not have you to be ignorant, brethren, concerning them which are asleep, that ye sorrow not, even as others which have no hope.

Job said "Also now, behold, my witness is in heaven, and my record is on high" (Job 16:19).

Sister Tracey had the same attributes of two of the servants in these passages!

SHE RECOGNIZED HER RESPONSIBILITY!

The master in this text went far away and entrusted three of his servants with something very precious to him. Two of them were responsible stewards.

They recognized the importance of their assignment and didn't take it lightly. In the same manner Tracey was a servant of the Lord who recognized her assignment, and she took it seriously.

She had a covenant with God and a contract with Grace!

Tracey was the ultimate Christian worker! She laid it all on the line for the Lord. Local shelters benefited from her work. Halfway houses were recipients of her many kind and benevolent deeds, and our church certainly profited from her selfless service, but make no bones about it, she was working for God and God alone! Our church just reaped the benefits.

ILLUSTRATION

My dear friend the late Bishop C.L. Sparks and I used to travel together all across this country together and on one occasion while visiting with a friend who pastored in Little Rock, an invaluable lesson on performing for an audience of one was displayed by a gourmet chef named Ms. Moncrief. She fed us and the other guest ministers like we were kings for 5 nights during that old fashioned revival service. One person tried to rain on her parade, telling her how the pastor and the church members didn't appreciate her. They even told her she may never see these out-of-town preachers ever again. She emphatically said yes, you may be right, but you missed the point. I'm not cooking for preachers, I'm cooking for God, they are just reaping the benefits. So it was with Tracey, her commitment was to God, the rest of us just reaped the collateral benefits of her kindness and generosity.

REALIZE HER ABILITY

Two of the servants were productive with what they had! God wants us to use our gifts for good and for his glory!

Tracey used her talent, time, and treasure as a faithful servant of God! This week the Chicago Sun Times did a profound article on Tracey's life and they quoted Yolanda Wells, our director of our mission. "She was so giving, even though she didn't have a lot of material things, she was always trying to give to others."

She stewarded God's gifts with grace, embodying a spirit of devotion and selflessness. She utilized her talents and resources to uplift others, inspire her community, and serve the Lord with unwavering faith.

ILLUSTRATION

She gave of herself! She was adamant about our church doors remaining open during the global pandemic! She told me " if doctors, nurses, grocery workers, truck drivers and postal workers were essential workers, certainly the church is essential. If there ever was a time people needed hope it was now during the pandemic, she insisted.

She didn't hide in her house and urge me to mask up and step out on faith, actually she was on the front line in the trenches with me, helping our church run safely during the height of COVID-19, when it reopened with capacity restrictions. "She risked her health to make sure our church doors were open!

RECORD OF ACCOUNTABILITY

In this parable, the master left for a while and later came back. Likewise, Jesus is coming back. You'd better believe that!

When he comes again there will be a day of accountability that awaits us all.

All of our collective hearts are heavy today, but let us somehow find solace in knowing that we don't have to worry about Tracey. (Tracey laid it all on the line for Christ) She gave life everything that she had.

ILLUSTRATION

Do you know where the wealthiest place on earth is? It's not the US Federal Reserve Bank! It's not the oil fields of Iran, Iraq, or Kuwait! And it's not the diamond minds of South Africa. We are headed to the wealthiest place on the planet when we leave here. It is the cemetery. There lie buried companies that were never started, inventions that were never made, bestselling books that were never written, and masterpieces that were never painted. In the cemetery is buried the greatest treasure of untapped potential."

Don't die old, die empty. That's the goal of life. Go to the cemetery and disappoint the graveyard. Tracey will be missed, she was invaluable! She left us at 55, but she gave us her all.

The Takeaway

REWARDED FOR HER ACTIVITY

Let nobody kid you, our fore-parents were on point. Only what you do for Christ will last!

She will hear the Lord say well done!

ILLUSTRATION

Before they came up with electronic deposit, payday was always the easiest day to go to work! Ain't no day like payday! Back in the day most of us wouldn't dare miss work on pay day. One of things that inspire me about working for the Lord is knowing that payday is coming. Well, I read somewhere that God is an amazing paymaster!

The Tomb of the Unknown soldier is in Arlington National Cemetery. The following words are inscribed on the tomb of the Unknown Soldier: "Here Rests In Honored Glory An American Soldier Known But To God."

If America remembers her unknown soldiers, think of the celebration that awaits countless servants of God who are relatively unknown on earth when they reach Heaven's gates. The Tomb of the Unknown soldier is at Arlington National Cemetery.

The following words are inscribed on the tomb of the Unknown Soldier: "Here Rests In Honored Glory An American Soldier Known But To God."

THANK GOD FOR THIS FAITHFUL SERVANT!

Family in the midst of your tears! I want you to know, you can make it!

I know it's dark right now! But you can make it! The chilly winds of life are blowing and the storms are raging, but you can make it! I know you're hurting but you can make it! Children right now you can't see your way, but I want you to know today that you can make it!

I've witnessed a global collapse in my life! I've witnessed the greatest terrorist attack of the 20th century while my wife and I were vacationing in another country! I lived to see a country that once enslaved blacks elect a black man as president! I've seen a country legalize a drug that destroyed black families and its on the brink of making white billionaires. I've seen so much! But there is one thing I've never seen! I've never seen the righteous forsaken, nor His seed begging for bread. Trust in the one who was born outside the inn! Trust in the one who was Raised in Nazareth and Baptized in the muddy Jordan River! Trust in that one who was crucified by the empire, yet raised by the power of God.

THE EULOGY FOR
PASTOR JOHN COLLINS

Then Jonathan said to David, "Tomorrow is the New Moon feast. You will be missed, because your seat will be empty.
I Samuel 20:18

The Title:

He Will Be Missed!

It's been a great honor to have Pastor John Collins as a friend! Thank you to the Collins family and Great True Vine Church for sharing this mighty man of God with us all. He had a great spirit! He was in a class by himself. We will miss his spirit. He was also a great supporter.

The Tribune

There is a reason every institution in our city and country is represented today at his home going celebration! Me being a civil rights leader, whether it was rallies, protests or press conferences, I could always depend on him to show up. Some people will look you square in the eye and tell you they will attend an event and know they were lying when they told you. Pastor Collins on the contrary if he gave you his word he was coming, you could take it to the bank! That uncommon support that he consistently provided will be missed!

Pastor Collins' shout was so unique! I loved to see and hear him shout. He brought incredible energy to a worship service. We visited him at the hospital during his last days on earth, and although we tried to distract him and change the subject, he would make subtle references to his earthly demise. One thing he told us was that he wanted a spirit-filled homegoing service.

His joy and enthusiasm in worship were truly special, a testament to his deep faith and passion for praising God like it was his last time. Even in his final days, he remained focused on his spiritual journey and the legacy he wanted to leave behind. He didn't shy away from discussing his departure from these mundane shores, instead expressing his wish for a celebration of life that was vibrant and filled with the Holy Spirit. He wanted his homegoing service to reflect the same energy and fire that characterized his life, ensuring that those who gathered to honor him would feel uplifted and inspired.

The Takeaway

As I reflect on the fiery praiser that my dear brother was, I'm reminded of a lady who went to her job one Friday. She reached in her mailbox to get her time card to punch in and instead found a note stating that her employment was terminated, and the old lady immediately began to shout! She began passionately jumping up and down! The old lady left her job and got in her car and had an accident that totaled her vehicle, and once again the old lady began to enthusiastically jump up and down, screaming glory to God. The old lady made it home only to discover that her house was on fire. The firemen were bringing out body bags as she arrived on site. In the midst of this madness, You know what the old lady did? She began to jump up and down all over again! She went to a revival at church Monday night and the moment service started, she started jumping up and down.

Her actions were repeated Monday, Tuesday, Wednesday, Thursday and Friday. That Friday night, on her way out one of the deacons saw her and pulled her to the side. He asked her how in the world can you be shouting and jumping after all you've been through? The old lady said you're educated and you can spell jump! The deacon said," of course J.U.M.P." The old lady said that's exactly how you spell jump, and the reason I'm jumping is because Jesus Understands My Problem. No matter what I face, I know Jesus Understands My Problem, and Jesus Understands My Praise! Family, we can make it! Gods got our back!

The only reason the Collins family shout, jump and praise God today during their dad and grandfather's homegoing service is that He instilled in them a deep faith. They have the assurance that to be absent from the body is to be present with the Lord. They know that Pastor is now dancing and shouting on Hallelujah Boulevard!

THE EULOGY FOR MONIQUE KING

Finally, my brethren, be strong in the Lord, and in the power of his might. Put on the whole armour of God, that ye may be able to stand against the wiles of the devil. For we wrestle not against flesh and blood, but against principalities, against powers, against the rulers of the darkness of this world, against spiritual wickedness in high places.
Ephesians 6:10-12, KJV

The Title:

Stand Your Ground!

Today is an incredibly difficult day. Grieving is a natural part of loss, and it's important that we acknowledge the weight of that reality. It would be abnormal to try to bypass the deep sorrow that comes with saying goodbye to someone we love. We are not happy today—a beautiful soul has been taken from us far too soon.

Yet, because of who Monique was, the impact she made, and the selfless life she lived, we gather not only to mourn her passing but also to celebrate her remarkable life. It's a Wonderful life!

Monique was a woman of deep faith, enduring strength, and unwavering conviction. Through her 58 year journey, she showed us the power of standing firm in God's truth, even in the face of life's greatest challenges.

To stand your ground means to remain firm and resolute in the face of challenges, opposition and adversity, chaos, catastrophes and chaos of life.

ILLUSTRATION

She wouldn't let anything stop her, I mean anything!

A few years ago, Monique was diagnosed with arthritis, which prevented her from working as consistently as she once had.

But in true Monique fashion, she didn't let that stop her. She adapted, becoming creative and ultimately finding a way to work from home. She made necessary adjustments but never gave in. She made concessions, but she never quit.

Her life teaches us three profound lessons that reflect her character, her faith, and her dedication to standing her ground in the Lord. Today, as we grieve, we also hold onto these lessons, cherishing the ways Monique touched our lives and the example she leaves behind.

The Tribute

MONIQUE STOOD HER GROUND FOR HER FAMILY

She was down for her family! Monique was totally devoted to her family. She was their rock, always going the extra mile, even when faced with her own struggles. Whether she was offering support, or just a loving presence, her family could always count on her to be there. She stood her ground for them, giving selflessly and tirelessly.

Her strength came from her deep faith, and through her love, she showed what it means to be truly committed to those you care about.

Illustration

On June 21st, Monique celebrated her mother's last birthday with her, and it was a day no one will forget. Only Monique had the capacity to unite her entire family and the dedication to make it happen. She brought everyone together—siblings, nieces, nephews, and cousins. Family members traveled from Atlanta, Alabama, and Mississippi, many of whom hadn't been to Chicago in years. But Monique made it happen, and she pulled it off with her characteristic grace and love.

Monique Stood Her Ground for Her Friends

Monique had a heart so big that it touched countless lives. She stood her ground for her friends, showing up for them in ways that made a lasting impact. Her kindness, her laughter, and her deep understanding of others made her a beloved figure in the lives of so many. In a world where it's easy to turn away from the needs of others, Monique stood firm, supporting and loving her friends through the ups and downs of life. Her love for people was rooted in her belief in God and her desire to live out His love. You know you are a smooth operator when you got 25 best friends!

Illustration

Monique had a heart so big that everybody wanted to claim her as their best friend. At first, I was like, "How you got 25 best friends?" But then something whispered to me, "Oh yes, you can. When you treat people right, when you're there for them when life gets tough, when you've always got their back and show love with no cap, folks will always see you as their best friend—even if they haven't been a best friend to you.

Proverbs 18:24 states, "A man that hath friends must shew himself friendly: and there is a friend that sticketh closer than a brother."

Monique Stood Her Ground for Her Faith

Most importantly, Monique stood her ground for her faith. She understood the spiritual battle described in Ephesians 6:10-12—that we are fighting not just against people, systems, policies, or economic inequities, but against the forces of darkness, spiritual wickedness, and evil in high places. Monique was not afraid. She fought spiritually, emotionally, mentally, and psychologically, embodying the full armor of God.

Even in the face of her tragic death, Monique remained a true warrior for Christ. I had the honor of meeting her 20 years ago and the privilege of being her pastor for many of those years. She understood who the real enemy was and never wavered in her faith. Like all of us, Monique had her faults. Well join the crowd.

Just like David, Moses, Rahab, Sarah, and yes, even Ira Acree, she fell short of the glory—but she never abandoned her faith.

The Takeaway

Monique is no longer with us, but her fight continues through us. She has run her race, and now, she rests in the presence of God, being rewarded for her faithful service.

We will miss her, but we take comfort knowing that she is in a better place. So, as we say goodbye, let us remember her example and continue to stand our ground—just as Monique did.

Don't be afraid to demand justice for the coward that took her life!

Rest easy, dear sister. We'll see you again. I want you to know that we will speak up for you! I'm not afraid to take a stand. What can they do to me? I'm not intimidated by thugs! You don't start nothing then it won't be nothing!

I'm not intimidated by the NRA! I will continue to advocate for getting guns off the streets and ensuring that background checks are mandatory.

Repeat after me: Put The Guns Down!

We will speak for Monique, but don't worry about her, you'd better worry about yourself. As the scripture says, "If they do this to the green tree, what will they do to the dry?"

ILLUSTRATION

An old preacher was once asked, after he had eulogized a dear friend and multiple members of his congregation in just a matter of months, what gave him the strength to go on. He shared a vision he had where he conversed with Death. The first question he asked Death was how long he had been around and how long he had held this job. Death responded that it had been since the beginning of time.

The preacher then asked, "Mr. Death, do you ever feel guilty about how you hurt people and cause families so much pain? You take the young and old, the rich and poor, princes and paupers. You separate husbands from their wives and wives from their husbands." Death replied, "No, not at all."

The old preacher continued, asking Death if he had ever made a mistake in all the centuries he had been in business. Death looked at the old preacher and said, "Although I've been at it for a long time and have taken people from all walks of life, I can confess that there was one time I made a mistake. It was more than 2000 years ago, with three men on a hill. I grabbed the one on the right, and he succumbed to my authority. I then grabbed the one on the left, and he too succumbed to the power of death. But when I came back to grab the man in the middle, he grabbed me back. We started wrestling and tumbling. We fought for three days, and eventually, I had to let him go!"

I came by today to share this as we fight for justice for Monique. That's why I'm not afraid of those who sit in positions of power! I work for the man in the middle of Calvary! He's been with me all the way. Family, I want you to know He will be with you—not some of the way, not a part of the way, but all the way. He promised never to leave me alone!

The End

ABOUT THE AUTHOR

Pastor Ira J. Acree has pastored Greater St. John Bible Church on Chicago's West Side for 35 years. He is a tireless advocate for empowerment, championing principles of entrepreneurship, education, economics, and evangelism. He holds a Bachelor of Arts in Political Science from the University of Illinois at Chicago and a Master of Arts in Christian Ministry from North Park Theological Seminary, where he received the Most Distinguished Alumni Award in 2020.

Most people know him for his social justice work within Chicago's activist community. Although writing books, leading his congregation, and spending time with his family keep him very busy, Acree has still managed to stay at the forefront of justice on issues of local and national relevance for the last 25 years. He has two adult children, Marcus (35) and Nicole (32), and he has been married to the former Miss Margaret Hill for 36 years. He is the author of three books: Man in the Mirror, In Pursuit of Mr. Right, and Just Do It. Acree is also the CEO of Absolute Results Consulting LLC.

Direct comments or requests to:

Pastor Ira J. Acree
Greater St. John Bible Church
1256 N. Waller Ave
Chicago, IL 60651
(773) 378-3300

About the Publisher

Let Life to Legacy bring your story to literary life! We offer the following publishing services: manuscript development, editing, transcription services, ghost-writing, cover design, copyright services, ISBN assignment, worldwide distribution, and eBook conversion. Throughout production, we keep the author informed every step of the way. Even if you do not have a manuscript, that's not a problem for us. We can ghost-write your book from audio recordings or legible handwritten documents. Whether print on demand or trade publishing, we have packages to meet your publishing needs. At Life to Legacy, we take the stress out of becoming a published author. Unlike other so-called publishers, we do more than just print books. Our books and eBooks are distributed to book buyers, distributors, and online retailers throughout the world. This is real publishing! Call us today for a free quote.

Please visit our website
www.Life2Legacy.com
or call us
708-272-4444
Send email inquiries
Life2Legacybooks@att.net

www.ingramcontent.com/pod-product-compliance
Lightning Source LLC
Chambersburg PA
CBHW020006290326
41935CB00007B/319